CARLO MARIA MARTINI

BIBLICAL MEDITATIONS

CARLO MARIA MARTINI

JESUS
WHY HE SPOKE IN PARABLES

COVENTRY
PRESS

Published in Australia by
Coventry Press
www.coventrypress.com.au
33 Scoresby Road Bayswater VIC 3153
an imprint of Freedom Publishing Books
www.freedompublishingbooks.com.au

ISBN 9780648323334

English translation copyright © Coventry Press 2018

First published in Italy entitled *Perché Gesù parlava in parabole? Meditazioni* by Edizioni Dehoniane 1985

Re-published by
© 2017 Edizioni San Paolo s.r.l.
Piazza Soncino 5 - 20092 Cinisello Balsamo (Milano) - ITALIA
www.edizionisanpaolo.it

All rights reserved. Other than for the purposes and subject to the conditions prescribed under the Copyright Act, no part of this publication may be reproduced, stored in a retrieval system, or transmitted in any form or by any means, electronic, mechanical, photocopying, recording or otherwise, without the prior permission of the publisher.

Scripture quotations are from the New Revised Standard Version Bible: Anglicised Catholic Edition, copyright © 1989, 1993, 1995 the Division of Christian Education of the National Council of the Churches of Christ in the United States of America.

Catalogue-in-Publication entry is available from the National Library of Australia http://catalogue.nla.gov.au

Printed in Australia by Brougham Press

CONTENTS

AN INVITATION	9
INTRODUCTION	13
In conversation with our inner Teacher	13
Choice of theme	15
Solitude and communication	18
Three Events	21
THREE FORMS OF GOSPEL KERYGMA	25
What is the kerygma?	25
The Church's preaching: three forms of the one kerygma	27
Quid hoc ad evangelium?	32
My gospel	34
JESUS PREACHED THE KERYGMA	37
With Jesus as our Teacher	38
The parables in Jesus' preaching	42
Questioning the Teacher	47
PARABLES OF THE SEED	51
The five parables of the seed: a *lectio* of Mark 4:1-9	52
Starting points for *meditatio*	58
The audience: those who heard the parables	61
Jesus' heart	63

THE POWER OF THE PARABLES OF THE SEED	67
The specific power of parable	68
Parables of the seed: urgency and involvement	73
Parable and me	76
Particular examination	78
The parables of judgement	81
The seventeen parables	82
Basic themes	88
Who are the parables told to?	89
Why did Jesus tell them?	90
Inner vigilance	92
Why Jesus Spoke in Parables	95
What parable is	95
Why Jesus could speak in parables	97
The importance of lectio divina	100
A simple example of lectio divina	106
The Parables of the Lost and Found	111
Parables told and parables lived	112
An audience with a jaundiced eye	116
A disconcerting revelation of God	118
In-house envy	123
JESUS' LIFE AS A PARABLE	127
Mashál and parabolé	127
Jesus, parable of God's tender love	129
The parable of the pierced side	132

Looking at the world from the Cross	137
PARABLES OF THE CALL	139
Call and invitation	139
Characteristics of the invitation	143
Kingdom business	146
Invitation to the wedding	148
Mission and vocation work and ministry	149
PARABLE, EUCHARIST, LIFE IN THE SPIRIT	153
Parable and Eucharist	154
Significance of the Eucharistic Congress	157
Parable and life in the Spirit	160
'Until all of us come to the unity of faith'	162

AN INVITATION

Why did Jesus speak in parables? This is the question that brings together the reflections in this book, all of them going back to August 1985. They were offered in the context of a retreat preached by Cardinal Martini in Kenya, and addressed to male and female missionaries. The meditations are once again testimony to his immediate but profoundly practical and evocative style. Their immediacy is not simply the result of the context (we are dealing with content transcribed from a recording, without the author having reviewed it), but a distinctive feature of a spiritual proposal capable of speaking to the most ordinary, everyday experience.

This is a profoundly sincere and sincerely provocative Martini, who asks himself about the parables, their relevance at a time like ours that no longer uses them, and in which 'speaking about God is hard work, tiring and hesitating.' Although, on the one hand, the focus of the Cardinal's attention is Jesus' communicative style, on the other, his interest shifts naturally to what speaking in parables means for us today: for our life, for our way of speaking of and with God. The connection is clear: 'Is my speaking about God *really me*? Is my speaking about God the normal continuation of who I am, of my being alive? Or is it 'me' on the one hand, and 'me speaking about God' on the other, when necessary, so that the two are distinct and different realities not always perfectly in agreement and fused together? These and other questions give rise to the desire to ask Jesus: how did you speak of God and why did you speak in parables?'

By way of response, Martini first of all offers some meditations of a fundamental nature that are a true and proper catechesis on forms of the kerygma which, at least initially, seem to be far from the usual biblical-flavoured pastoral style used by the Archbishop of Milan. Except, we then discover that the point of convergence is always there, compelling and drawing us in: 'What is my gospel for my personal situation? What, right now, expresses the joy God gives me or that I expect in view of the revealed mystery?... In need of communion and, so to say, distressed by my loneliness, I discover that my fullness is given to me by God himself. He is the gospel of divine communication.'

Jesus is direct testimony to this gospel, especially through the parables. The Cardinal immediately clarifies that they 'are in no way a gentle teaching: rather are they weapons of war, moments of struggle, cries that arise from deep, inner emotion, however veiled and pedagogically well-dispensed they may be. The world of the parables allows us to penetrate Jesus' power in communicating the mystery of God, and also his wisdom, attention to the other, his irony, humour and ability to navigate difficult situations without awkwardness and with great elegance. It is a way of coming to know the mystery of God in Christ revealed to human beings.'

The 'power' of the parables is summed up in their capacity to engage us, to find their roots in a real situation, to focus elements and symbols, conferring on the bare word 'the power of a battering ram that demolishes its target through involvement rather than by direct blow.' Jesus can use the parables so that, in the gap between the history of the world and the mystery of the kingdom, God's history with human beings can be told: there is a 'history of God' that Jesus knows and he can be its narrator, mediator and the one who meditates upon it. His very life is a parable of the tender love of God our Father. Martini emphasises this by going back through the numerous gospel parables (the seed, on judgement, the call, the lost and found) with his Socratic questioning wisdom. He does this convincingly.

After all, there is but one secret: learning to look at the world as Christ did, so we can imitate his way of telling its story. Or – and it is the same thing – learning to situate oneself from the perspective of the cross, the 'perfect' parable for 'looking at the world, history, our community, our personal and pastoral problems, having understood something of the Father's *profound mercy*.'

Giuseppe Mazza

INTRODUCTION

In conversation with our inner Teacher

It is certainly cause for great joy to find myself here, both to meet you and, above all, to be able to get to know you and pray with you. I consider it an immense gift of the Lord to share this experience of prayer with so many missionaries, women and men, because in some way, a large part of the missionary community in Kenya and also neighbouring countries is symbolically represented here.

Clearly, along with joy, there is some trepidation: missionaries are the forward scouts of the Church, and rather than teaching, I should be listening and learning from you. If this fear does not deter me, it is due to two consolations I receive from the words of Scripture.

The first is in Matthew's Gospel:

> When they hand you over, do not worry about how you are to speak or what you are to say; for it is not you who speak, but the Spirit of your Father speaking through you (10:19-20).

It is true that these words refer to someone brought before the courts, but they also refer to giving witness, to *martyría*. Insofar as I am giving witness, I trust that the Holy Spirit will suggest what I might say.

The second consolation I take from John's Gospel:

> But the Advocate, the Holy Spirit, whom the Father will send in my name, will teach you everything, and remind you of all that I have said to you (14:26).

Here, Jesus' promise is not limited to the moment of martyrdom or appearance before the courts: it is a promise for the Christian, for everyone. I would call this second consolation *the inner Teacher*. It is not the person addressing you now who is teaching, but your inner Teacher. This is a most important truth and perhaps one I did not give much thought to until recently. At the beginning of July, we made a retreat with the bishops of Lombardy in preparation for the anniversary of St Augustine's conversion (which took place in Milan in 386). I was very much struck, during the retreat, by the fundamental Augustinian notion of the 'inner Teacher'. Everything being said was just to remind us of what, in reality, the Teacher was saying inwardly to each of us. That is particularly so for you who already know the Christian faith well in all its aspects. So I will only be calling to mind one or other aspect, to open up echoes of your direct inner conversation.

A retreat, then, can be described just this way: a conversation with our inner Teacher. We should experience this amazing reality much more often, as St Augustine did. When faced with any problems (we read about it in his *Confessions*, in his sermons, in his way of speaking to the people), he began to pray: Lord, I did not understand this passage of Scripture; what did you want to say? Teach me. I do not see how to resolve this problem: what are you, the supreme Truth, telling me?

Each day, we should experience the certainty that the 'supreme truth' of God is in us. It speaks to us in Jesus and through the grace of the Holy Spirit, and it reveals, informs us, allows us to understand what we, our ministry, our life needs. We are often upset or disturbed by the effort to resolve a problem, be it pastoral or practical, and forget to abandon ourselves first of all to a conversation with our inner Teacher.

So, let us make use of the retreat to take up many of the problems once more that have worried us during the year – the problems of community life or relationships with others, problems of pastoral engagement or apostolic activity – and make them the object of a conversation. The retreat is precisely this conversation with our Teacher, beginning from our actual set of circumstances, listening once more to the words of Scripture and the Church that our inner Teacher suggests to us *in the way best suited to us*.

Choice of theme

The theme I thought of developing in these meditations could seem strange. Initially, topics of broad interest came to mind. The Acts of the Apostles, the life of the early Church, and others. But suddenly, and irresistibly, I felt I should plan something different, something that I can pose as a question: *why did Jesus speak in parables?* It could seem a simplistic question or an exegetical problem; instead, it is much more than that.

It is important, first of all, to stress the fact that Jesus spoke in parables. Indeed, there are some almost paradoxical statements in the four Gospels: it would seem that we can deduce from these that Jesus only spoke in parables. In Mark's Gospel, for example, at the end of the chapter on the parables, we read: 'With *many* such parables he spoke the word to them, as they were able to hear it; he did not speak to them except in parables' (4:33-34).

The statement in Mark is picked up by John, and is significant. In fact, the Fourth Gospel does not pick up on or follow the Synoptic Gospels, but it does so on this point, though it uses another term, and it increases the prescription, so to speak. I am talking about Jesus' final words before the great prayer of Chapter 17 (after which comes the passion):

> I have said these things to you in figures of speech. The hour is coming when I will no longer speak to you in figures, but will tell you plainly of the Father (16:25).

One could object: So? You are about to finish your preaching, and now you begin saying you will no longer speak in figures! Clearly, it was very important for Jesus to speak this way, because just as he was about to go to his passion, he thinks of his whole life as a discourse given in parables.

So Jesus spoke in parables. In Europe, at least, we do not; we are unaccustomed to expressing ourselves in parables. We repeat Jesus' parables in our ordinary preaching as if they were brief moralising examples (and we will see they are not!), however, we do not know how to create new ones.

I asked myself why I do not use parables when I speak to the people. I have asked myself if it is my mistake, or if our tastes have changed by comparison with Jesus' times. And I have understood that this is a question to be explored, better understood.

The problem would not be so serious if it did not touch on one that is very serious: in Europe, we struggle to speak about God; in the Western world, speaking about God is hard work, tiring and hesitating. We categorise ourselves as 'verticalists' or 'horizontalists'. The first group always wants an open, evangelical discourse about God. The other group, on the other hand, want it expressed in life, through charity and service, mentioning God very little in order not to create division among people, not to cause confusion and misunderstanding. The truth is that we experience a certain awkwardness in tackling this subject. Hence, the need, the desire to understand how Jesus spoke about God. Why did Jesus also speak in parables, through figures of speech?

I think the situation may be better in Africa, where probably the parable is held in high esteem, at least the figure of speech, the proverb, figurative ways of expressing things. The parable corresponds to the mentality of the African people. Yet, I believe there is no shortage of problems, and over these days, asking one or other missionary, I have felt this to be the case when I query why people ask for baptism. The answers have been interesting and diverse; and they have allowed me to sense how much of an effort is needed to achieve the full clarity of the gospel, of God's revelation.

I have also asked myself what the missionary's language should be like, what form it should take. The problem is an old one, and goes back to the beginning of the missions. Perhaps it could be profitable to reconsider the question here, not as a lesson or a discussion but, as St Augustine did, as a prayer: 'Lord, you who are the Truth, show me what is true. Lord, guide me in your truth. Speak to me, you who are wisdom; put the right thoughts and words in my heart, not for myself but so I can nourish my brothers and sisters.'

I have explained to you why I felt the theme on which we will be meditating was urging me on inwardly; there were reasons involving our Western mentality; reasons inherent in our mission situation, and reasons of a personal nature that I will express with this further question: Is my speaking about God *really me*? Is my speaking about God the normal continuation of who I am, of my being alive? Or is it 'me' on the one hand, and 'me speaking about God' when necessary, on the other, so that they are two distinct and different realities not always in perfect agreement and fused together? These and other questions give rise to the desire to ask Jesus: how did you speak of God and why did you speak in parables?

Each of you could then formulate your own questions. In general, at the beginning of a retreat, it is good to bring out the questions we have within, questions that come from our experience of the year past and how things have especially given us joy in the Lord, or have created difficulties. Retreat time is the best time for placing myself before God as I am, with the problems, questions and anxiety I feel most keenly, in reference to my being, my Christianity, my religious life, my way of living. It will then be easier to truthfully engage in dialogue with our inner Teacher, comparing ourselves with what the pages of the gospel can tell us.

Solitude and communication

One practical pointer seems to me to be useful. In itself, the retreat is a time for silence and solitude: nevertheless it is a solitude whose purpose is to deepen our capacity for communication, removing it from its superficiality, its wordiness – often its insignificance – to give it depth. And it is important to set this as a goal: to deepen our innate capacity for communication through solitude; in fact, we are individuals insofar as we are communicative.

We should experience a threefold communication at retreat time:

1. *Communication with God.* The fruitfulness of these days depends on our ability to rediscover the ease of communication with God, the pleasure of speaking with him, of conversing. We need to rediscover this as a fresh, affectionate, joyful and nurturing source. Sometimes, during the year, our prayer is an effort, due to tiredness or lack of time, and perhaps, because of this we put it off. So, we should rediscover the rivers of living water that Jesus promises, flowing from the hearts of believers (Jn 7:38), letting them flow from the wellspring of our inner prayer.

It is true that prayer is a grace to ask of the Lord, a necessary gift in order not to fall into indifference, atheism or paganism, or just the mechanics of our service. Nevertheless, our readiness to accept this gift depends on our good will. So, we need to try to rebuild the conditions (physical, mental, spiritual) for this wellspring to be opened or to open itself.

For some, or for many, the moment that disposes us will be adoring humility, especially in the silent, prolonged adoration of the Eucharist, or in an act of humility before praying.

For others or on other occasions, it will be a simple conversation with the Lord, starting out from his word, perhaps just a single word that has struck us, or we can take our cue from something in our lives that we reinterpret in this conversation: perhaps it is a conversation that struggles a bit, without many words initially, but one that gradually leads us to breathe the divine mystery.

For still others, it will be an examination of conscience or a reflection on a prayer we usually say, like the *Our Father*; or it may be simply going for a walk, contemplating nature in calm and serenity, slowly re-balancing our thoughts.

We all do things in our own way, but it is the serious responsibility of us all not to ignore the source, to learn to know ourselves and to know through which dispositions, including physical (body posture) and mental ones (silence, reading, adoration, our inner song), the Lord is calling on us to communicate with him.

2. Communication with the retreat master. The retreat master is not properly called the 'preacher', because after a homily the preacher leaves each to their own thoughts. Instead, the retreat master must walk with the retreatant through a daily conversation.

Given the number of people taking part in this retreat, it is materially impossible to do this here; however, there are three ways this communication can take place:

– The direct, spoken method for those who want it, and within the time constraints;

– In writing: a question or a doubt or something that can help you express yourself before God. Often the fact of writing to someone about what we have within is a very great help for opening ourselves to dialogue with the Lord, for asking for spiritual enlightenment or to formulate a prayer. And it is a real way of communicating.

– Communal communication: in the evening, we are free to meet, to exchange what the Lord has granted each one, what the Lord has had the individual understand, the reflections he has aroused in us.

3. *Communication with the Church.* Solitude over these days should deepen our communication with the Church by internalising things and by contemplation of an ecclesial kind.

The way of internalisation is the certainty that *right now*, in the secrecy of my dialogue with God, the destinies of the Church, the world, people entrusted to me, non-Christians, Christians in difficulty, the sick, the suffering, all come into play. By responding to the Lord's call and his request for a decision for him, I am taking on all the problems of the Church. The Church moves forward if I move forward, the kingdom of God grows if I say yes now.

The way of ecclesial contemplation is the certainty of living out my choice before God in communication with the whole Church, especially beginning from the Church triumphant: Our Lady, the angels, saints, our protectors, those who have gone before us in the kingdom (parents, relatives, friends). There always is, but especially at retreat time, a time of solitude, a shared presence of the Church, and it is good to express it in prayer, conversing with the saints, with Our Lady. Our brothers and sisters who are now with God are in fact interested in the things that were entrusted to them during their lives and will talk with us about them and intercede for us. Therefore, we can experience our inner journey as being immersed in the whole reality of God's kingdom. Each of us becomes a focus of this kingdom, responsible for it, when we listen to the Word.

Three Events

Finally, I would like to recall three events that mark our retreat:

– The Eucharistic Congress in Nairobi;

– The anniversary of Vatican Council II, with the upcoming Extraordinary Synod of Bishops;

– The anniversary of the conversion of St Augustine, because he was a saintly African and probably the greatest Doctor of the Church of all time.

How do we keep these three events in mind during the retreat? By referring to three very simple considerations:

– With regard to the Eucharistic Congress, every now and again we should say, when listening to Jesus speaking in parables: how is this reflected in the Eucharist? The Eucharist is at the centre of Christian life, and every reality of Christian life has its reflection in the Eucharist.

– With regard to Vatican II, there would be so many elements to reflect on. One of the problems the Extraordinary Synod of Bishops must confront is the matter of correct interpretation of the Council. It is a question that returns persistently and is almost the essence of Cardinal Ratzinger's book: *Rapporto Sulla Fede (Report on the Faith)*. It also emerges from many other documents of recent times: the most recent being the submission of the Conference of Catholic Bishops in England and Wales in preparation for the Synod.

The problem is one we should take to heart while we listen to Jesus speaking in parables: we can be assisted by a correct interpretation of the central points that the Council's experience has partly resolved, partly illuminated. This has helped us understand what was emerging. Then, perhaps, things became clearer after the Council, or they were obscured through inadequate interpretation of the Council. We cannot possibly claim we are genuinely part of the Church today if we do not pose this question. It is the Pope himself who invites us to do so.

INTRODUCTION

– For the anniversary of St Augustine, we should try to experience his teaching about the 'inner Teacher', and understand better what his great contribution to the Church has been: the discovery of inwardness. The discovery, that is, that the entire world of gospel revelation finds its privileged place in the human heart, and that the heart of one human being is in relationship with the heart of all human beings, with the body of the Church. St Augustine is the master of inwardness and ecclesiality, and it is from this perspective that we want to be taught by him.

++++

I am thinking of offering the meditations in the following order:

– First, two meditations of a fundamental nature;

– Then we will run through some groups of parables to listen to Jesus speaking about a variety of topics, in such a way that we will then be able to reflect on Jesus' very words, asking him what he wanted to say to whomever was listening, and what he wants to say to us today.

– After each group of parables, we will compare their language to see how they reflect our life and faith. Let us entrust our resolutions to the Lord since he knows how to bring to completion, when and how he wants, what he suggests.

> 'We ask you, Lord
> to be our inner Teacher over these days.
> Grant that we may pray
> in union with the entire universal Church,
> aware that we are not here just for ourselves.

In the Barque of Peter, people are at work on all
   sides,
some struggling amid the storm,
trying to bail out water;
while we, by the grace of God,
have the opportunity to spend time
in silence,
rest, tranquillity,
even if it is a demanding time.
Lord, we want to spend it
in the name of the entire Church,
in the name of all Christians,
all catechumens, all communities,
all those we have present in our minds
at the moment.
We entrust them all to you,
including our Churches of origin
who are praying with us
and are always praying
for our missionary work.
Grant that we may be in and for your Church
the way you want us to be there. Amen.'

THREE FORMS OF GOSPEL KERYGMA

I am offering a meditation of a fundamental nature on the Church's preaching, starting with two words or so from Chapter 1 of Mark's Gospel where it says, after John the Baptist had been imprisoned: 'Jesus came to Galilee, *proclaiming the good news of God*' (v. 14).

I would like to try to break down the two main words which, in the Greek text, are *'kerùsson to evangélion,'* or 'kerygmatising the gospel.' First of all, we shall explore what we mean by kerygma and gospel; then we will ask ourselves if there really are three forms of gospel kerygma, and what questions the gospel kerygma puts to us; finally, we ask what *my* gospel is.

What is the kerygma?

You certainly know that the words 'kerygma' and 'gospel' do not always have a well-defined meaning. For our purposes we need to define them in a way that corresponds to what we want to emphasise.

Kerygma is the proclamation of a herald who cries out in a loud voice. It is often used in the New Testament to describe the proclamation of Jesus or the apostles, their preaching, above all, but not exclusively, the first preaching or first proclamation to the Gentiles. Of itself the word means 'public proclamation'; it is applied, then, to any kind of public proclamation.

Gospel means 'good news', a typical New Testament expression, the fundamental good news that is the core of the whole Christian event.

It is in this sense that I pose the question: Is there a *core part of the proclamation in the New Testament that can be called kerygma* in a privileged sense and can also be called gospel? Because 'kerygma' tells us the *way* of proclaiming it, while 'gospel' tells us its content: the proclamation of good news and the good news itself.

There certainly are some core statements in the New Testament. There are passages where the kerygma or gospel is proposed in a somewhat broader form, as in the addresses and discourses in the Acts of the Apostles. There are other passages where the proposal is put more briefly, more simply, reducing it almost to a single sentence. Clearly, Christianity cannot be summed up in one sentence; however, that sentence is a seed; it is like a proton or neutron that generates a whole atomic chain reaction. The New Testament has the awareness that it is possible, even useful, to lay out the Christian newness of its experience sometimes in a concise, very brief, incisive fashion.

For example, when St Paul says, in the Letter to the Romans: 'For I am not ashamed of the gospel; it is the power of God for salvation to everyone who has faith' (1:16), he is providing a summary: the gospel is God's power for the salvation of whoever believes. When explained, it would give us the entire preaching of the Apostle or at least, a good part of it. So also in the Letter to the Romans once more, we read: 'If you confess with your lips that Jesus is Lord (*Kyrios*) and believe in your heart that God raised him from the dead, you will be saved' (10:9). Here is another concise formula: Jesus is *Kyrios*, he is Lord; God has raised him from the dead.

Developed in the context of the New Testament, the formula is seminal, central, a vital nerve centre from which the other forms of the kerygma depart, the various forms of preaching. I have given two examples but you could find many other similar expressions.

In conclusion, by kerygma or gospel, we mean here the *core* of the Christian preaching.

The Church's preaching: three forms of the one kerygma

Is this core one or many? In itself, it is clearly one and can only be one. On this we have the very strong statement of Paul in his Letter to the Galatians:

> I am astonished that you are so quickly deserting the one who called you in the grace of Christ and are turning to a different gospel – not that there is another gospel but there are some who are confusing you and want to pervert the gospel of Christ. But even if we or an angel from heaven should proclaim to you a gospel contrary to what we proclaimed to you, let that one be accursed! As we have said before, so now I repeat, if anyone proclaims to you a gospel contrary to what you received, let that one be accursed! (1:6-9).

There is only one core of the gospel, which is Christ who died and was raised.

Just the same, the New Testament has a degree of multiplicity of kerygmas and gospels. The very fact that the four Gospels have that strange title *'according to'* (*'katà'* Luke, '*katà*' Matthew, etc.) indicates that the gospel is expressed in different ways, and these expressions not only respond to the desire to vary verbal formulas, but are applications of the one gospel to different times, needs and stages of the Christian experience. Hence the one gospel becomes many.

But this is not all. The circumstances and historical situations of the listener could require a certain kind of gospel, what Paul calls *my gospel*; 'Remember Jesus Christ, raised from the dead, a descendant of David – that is my gospel' (*katà to evangélion mou*, 2 Tim 2:8). Clearly it is the gospel of Jesus Christ raised from the dead; however, if Paul calls it 'my' gospel, it means there is something specific about it, as we see more clearly, for example, in the Letter to the Ephesians:

> This is the reason that I Paul am a prisoner of Christ Jesus for the sake of you Gentiles [here we see Paul's situation regarding the Gentiles] – for surely you have already heard of the commission of God's grace that was given me for you and how the mystery was made known to me by revelation, as I wrote above in a few words, a reading of which will enable you to perceive my understanding of the mystery of Christ (3:1-4).

The Apostle claims his own way of grasping the historical and saving moment, which for him is direct proclamation to the Gentiles, the unity of two peoples (Jews and Gentiles) into one. For him, then, the gospel becomes the way to proclaim God's mercy in Christ addressed directly to the Gentiles who are called to be part of the one people of God. This, we can say, is 'Paul's gospel'. It is the one gospel lived out in the historical situation of salvation, which is his experience of the time: it is spiritual and pastoral discernment that leads the Apostle to express the kerygma.

We can deduce from this that the kerygma is one, yet is expressed in a multiplicity of kerygmas and gospels. By way of a schematic summary, I would suggest the existence of at least three basic forms of kerygma (there are obviously many other intermediate forms).

1. First of all there is the *primary gospel* form, difficult to express in a precise catechetical formula. One could more or less say: *God freely offers salvation in Christ to me, a sinner.* God saves me the sinner, in Christ. In a nutshell, this is the first step, the elementary gospel, but it already contains all the essentials. So it is not enough to say that God is good, that Jesus is risen if we do not mean by this that God's goodness in Christ who died and was raised *offers salvation to me, a sinner.*

The gospel also includes the awareness of my sin, my inability to save myself, my need for salvation. God freely and mercifully comes to my aid in this through the death and resurrection of Jesus. It would be left to the *didaché* to explain this proclamation: 'In the Crucified one is your salvation.' While ignoring the Christological aspect, the publican in the Temple, for example, alludes to this: 'O God, be merciful to me, a sinner!' It presumes an awareness of God, his freely given mercy, of the need human beings have for salvation. If, as part of this awareness we include God's merciful act in the love of Christ which restores the human being, we have the primary formulation of the kerygma which all the other expressions of teaching and catechesis lead back to. A preaching or catechesis that does not reflect this truth sounds empty and false.

Another expressive form of this gospel, very well known in Eastern monastic practice, is the petition behind the 'Jesus Prayer': *Iesù Christé, Theou uié eléison emé amartolòn* – Jesus Christ, Son of God, have mercy on me, a sinner. It is a summary of the kerygma expressed before Christ crucified and risen. The Jesus Prayer nurtures our spiritual life precisely because it expresses the kerygma.

There can also be other formulations. Concretely, the first, elementary form of the kerygma is the act of contrition in the experience of someone approaching the Sacrament of Penance: may the merciful God accept me as a sinner in the blood of Christ and free me from my sin.

2. Is there a second formula, an improved one, which says the same truth in other words? The New Testament teaches us that there is, and we can put it concisely thus: *the new life of the Spirit*. It is a much more positive way of proclaiming the good news; the new life through the merciful grace of God that not only justifies penitent sinners, but sanctifies them in the fullness of the light and truth of being human.

The new life of the Spirit means that human beings are capable of loving with their entire being, of living the beatitudes and fruits of the Spirit: justice, joy, peace, kindness, patience, generosity... and of living in the full realisation of their humanity. It is complete salvation for the human person in the grace of the Spirit who comes from Christ crucified; so, it is another form of the kerygma which speaks of all the positive nature of the Christian experience. It reveals Christianity as responding to the deepest needs of the person and of humanity: the need for love, communication, truth, light, expansion.

This second form of the kerygma clearly assumes that forgiveness of sin has been obtained, that the old person has been conquered in the second baptism which is penitence, and that all the richness of evangelical humanity has then flourished. The New Testament, beginning with the Letter to the Romans (Chapter 8), has some marvellous descriptions of the new humanity born of the Holy Spirit.

3. *A third form* of the kerygma, even more exalted, is found in the Fourth Gospel. John places something at the centre of his proclamation that is difficult to put into words (which are always limited, each one needing lengthy explanation). One could sum it up in this formula: *Jesus with the Father. The human being is called to be one with the Father in Christ.* Here, we have the Trinitarian revelation: the human being is destined to be with the Son, to be with the Son in the Father. The same gospel is expressed here in the most sublime, if disconcerting, of ways.

++++++

I have sought to describe the three forms of the one kerygma by speaking to the single notion that Jesus died for my sins, that a new life in the Spirit is possible for me, and that I am called to share in the life of the Trinity. Just the same, it also needs to be formulated for the community as such.

First way: 'All this is from God, who reconciled us to himself through Christ' (2 Cor 5:18). The sin of the world is pardoned and taken up in Christ's cross; the world is reconciled with the Father; the Father offers reconciliation to humanity.

Second way: the new life of the Spirit is the life of the Church. The Church is the new humanity capable of regenerating relationships between people: charity, communion, communication (Acts 2:14).

According to the expression of Vatican II the Church, as a model of humanity, is the 'sacrament or sign of the unity of the whole human race' (LG, 1); it shows the world that the hope given it is one of coexistence called to communion, not human butchery.

Third way: expressed by Jesus himself: we are one with Christ in the Father; we are one body; we are not only an historical and visible body but an eternal one from now on, with Christ in the Father. We are already eternity, paradise begun, and what we are will never fail to be; our communication with the Father will not be interrupted by anything, not even by death. It will continue forever. The Church, then, is already the anticipation of the perfect knowledge of God.

Quid hoc ad evangelium?

The kerygma, or gospel as we have expressed it, is the source of questions about our entire Christian existence, questions which can be reduced to one basic one: *Quid hoc ad evangelium?* What does this have to do with the Gospel? The question can be extended to all aspects of our life, our apostolate, our way of being Church. It is simply a case of an application of the central nature of the gospel, of the primacy of the kerygma. If the gospel kerygma is truly the primary reality, the core of Christianity, then there is a need for our way of life, the Church's way of life, to be a reflection of that.

Sometimes, I invite priests (and I first invite myself!) to ask themselves after preaching: What was there of the gospel in my words? Have I perhaps only offered some advice or information, some tools? Was there at least a crumb of good news in what I just said? I recall someone asking me at a meeting: 'Why do you always ask: what has this to do with evangelisation?' And I replied that he had mistaken my words: evangelisation is a *function* of the Church, while the gospel ['*vangelo*' or even '*evangelo*' in Italian] is the fundamental core, and sums up the manifestation of God to me in Christ!

So, it is a very useful and appropriate exercise to ask ourselves often: what has everything I have done and said and thought today had to do with the gospel? It is equivalent to recognising the primacy of the Word, the primacy of Christ who reveals the Father, the perennial nature of this gospel, because we will be experiencing it, living it for all eternity, contemplating the Father who invites us to his life in Christ in the bond of love of the Spirit.

St Augustine often explains that when we arrive at contemplating something of the kerygma in prayer, meaning we feel the profound joy of our unity with the Father in Jesus, then we already have a foretaste of heavenly fullness. In the *Confessions*, for example in Chapter 9, he speaks of the ecstasy he experienced together with his mother Monica: very slowly conversing together, they went even more *into the beyond* and understood what unity with God meant. By seizing on a drop of what heavenly conversation is, they experienced the beginning of fullness.

On the other hand, all the Fathers of the Church focused their experience on the kerygma, and all their speculation was structured according to this expressive manner.

My gospel

Let us formulate the following questions: 'What is my gospel for my personal situation? What, right now, expresses the joy God gives me or that I expect in view of the revealed mystery?'

In fact, we always stand before a gospel; each of us does. But my life is not enlightened by it, nor unified nor strengthened by it unless I take hold of an actual form of the gospel *for me*. Perhaps it is a case of very simple things: if, for example, some misunderstandings between myself and others poison my life somewhat, hinder me or my achievement of a new life in Christ, or the certainty of being able to communicate once more in the grace of the Holy Spirit, then these things represent my gospel, which brings my life back on track.

We constantly need to be nourished by the gospel, to hear the Word of God as good news *for me now*. And, indeed, the fundamental Christian approach is the certainty that there is always a gospel, at any moment of human experience: even in prison, Paul says, there is the gospel.

There are many wonderful instances of this. For example, I visited a group of young prisoners two weeks ago, and had to reply to written questions they had sent me. One spoke of prison as a place of degradation, darkness, moral misery and asked me how, in my view, it could be possible to find the way to God in prison. After I had read out the question, one young man stood up and said that, despite everything, it was very possible to find God in prison and that he had found him. Then he told me about his experience and explained how he had come to discover God's mercy.

Perhaps it is precisely from such difficult situations that sometimes the most beautiful testimonies of the gospel of

God as salvation for sinners flow. Of course, Jesus himself reminded us that he came for sinners, and anyone who does not feel that he or she is a sinner and in need of salvation will find it difficult to accept the good news of Jesus. The gospel is for the poor, for those who feel they are not up to it, for those who feel they have no security in this world.

To understand what my gospel is, I must understand what my poverty is, my sin, my fragility, where God must save me. Salvation clearly can be very positive: communion with the Son and the Father, for example, is a gospel that supposes an entire journey. It is the end point of a journey of salvation and mercy. In need of communion and, so to say, distressed by my loneliness, I discover that my fullness is given to me by God himself. He is the gospel of divine communication.

> 'Lord, help me to understand
> which is my gospel,
> which are my gospels.
> Help me to recall,
> in memory, your great benefits,
> recall the sustaining moments
> of my spiritual experience.
> Lord, I seem to have no gospel:
> Help me to understand which gospel I need.
> Lord, I do not know how to pray;
> help me to understand
> that it is the Holy Spirit
> who gives me the grace to pray.
> Perhaps this is my gospel,
> the good news I am in need of:
> that the Spirit can pray in me

and that he gives me strength in my weakness,
in my inability to pray …
Thank you, Lord,
for showing yourself to me
through the merciful
and saving power of your gospel!'

JESUS PREACHED THE KERYGMA

'Father, grant that we may formulate the questions
that truly correspond to our desires.
May our questions
first of all express our desire for you,
the deepest desire in us.
May they express the desire for your glory,
your love, your truth,
your kingdom and your justice.
In posing these questions,
may we already enter into conversation with you
and receive your response
which is the communication of your life.
May these questions
not only be ours, but the Church's
and from people whom we love.
May they be the sign of the Church's attention
to you, the perfect and absolute truth
without which everything is dark
and through which everything receives light,
even the darkest parts of the earth.'

With this kind of faith and trust, having considered the preaching of the Church, especially of the primitive Church, we would now like to pose a question that could sound strange, almost irrelevant.

Did Jesus preach the kerygma? It might sound irrelevant, because if he did not preach the kerygma, then who did? Jesus himself is the gospel.

However, at least as a question for reflection, for better understanding, the question is posed: did Jesus preach the kerygma? If we read the Gospels, especially the Synoptics, we will struggle to find Jesus preaching the kerygma in any of the forms we have described. Jesus is not a preacher who can be predicted. We cannot say: his message is this, here he is saying it, repeating it. Jesus upsets our mental framework somewhat. Yet his life is divine and we must learn from him who God is, how God works and how one should live according to God.

So, we want to contemplate him – beginning from our question – and I will limit myself to outlining some pointers for a response, leaving you to a broader, more personal reflection.

With Jesus as our Teacher

1. First of all, there are some reasons for saying that Jesus did preach the kerygma, hence reasons for answering the question in the affirmative. *The affirmative answer* is one we can read in an already quoted verse in Mark: 'Jesus came to Galilee, proclaiming the good news of God' (1:14). So, he kerygmatised the gospel and there is no doubt that the early community, needing to summarise what the Master said, put it this way: *Jesus preached the good news*. Not only do we have the judgement of the early community, but we also know the words he preached with: 'The time is fulfilled, and the

kingdom of God has come near, repent, and believe the good news' (Mk 1:15).

Some exegetical issues arise here; are these really Jesus' words, or has the community summarised them? Is it Jesus who used the words 'good news' or the community that guessed them and got it right?

Leaving the exegetical question aside, we must, however, say that Jesus preached something similar to the gospel, the good news. Just the same, when we examine this verse of Mark's, we see that it differs from the forms of the kerygma we have laid out following St Paul, St John, the Acts of the Apostles. It is certainly not easy to say why the expression: '…. The time is fulfilled and the kingdom of God has come near, repent, and believe ….' is a gospel in the sense we have explained. Really, it is a rather complex formula and already poses some problems: in what way did Jesus preach the gospel? And especially: why did he not use any of the formulas (summaries) employed by the early church, which are still valid today?

The reasons for our 'Yes', then, suggest grounds for a broader reflection; or at least, for a degree of caution.

2. There are also reasons for giving a *negative response* to our question. We have said that according to the Gospels, Jesus often, indeed always, spoke in parables. Mark 4:34: 'He did not speak to them except in parables.'

Now the kerygma by nature is an open, clear, lucid proclamation, while the parable uses enigmatic, allusive language. Does this mean that Jesus did preach the kerygma but often used enigmatic, symbolic language? Understanding the figure of Jesus becomes more complex.

> To you has been given the secret of the kingdom of God [*he is speaking to the disciples*], but for those outside, everything comes in parables; in order that they may indeed look, but not perceive, and may indeed listen, but not understand; so that they may not turn again and be forgiven (Mk 4:11-12).

Here we are really thrown somewhat. It seems that Jesus does not want to openly proclaim the kingdom and even hides it, that open and clear preaching, the new life given in the Holy Spirit, is hidden, veiled, and accompanied by remarks on human blindness and lack of understanding.

Another passage that complicates our response is Mark 8:31-33, [following Peter's confession]:

> Then he began to teach them that the Son of Man must undergo great suffering and be rejected by the elders, the chief priests, and the scribes, and be killed, and after three days rise again. *He said all this quite openly.*

On the one hand, the comment 'He said this quite openly,' shows that Jesus did not always engage in open preaching of the kerygma. On the other hand (and this is where the complication arises), we see that the form of the word spoken openly is not strictly gospel: the Son of Man must be rejected and put to death. It is at this point that Peter no longer recognises Jesus' preaching and rebukes him: '... this must never happen to you!'

Already in the introduction we recalled the line in John 16:25:

I have said these things to you in figures of speech [the Greek word *paroimìais* also means proverbs, parables]. The hour is coming when I will no longer speak to you in figures.

For John, Jesus spoke in allusive forms that both say something and don't say something.

All of this is certainly unexpected, mysterious for us, and doesn't seem to be part of our image of Jesus openly and courageously preaching the kerygma, at least as we intend it at first sight.

If we read Chapter 1 of Acts we find another strange statement. The author says that in his first book (the Gospel according to Luke) he wrote about 'all that Jesus did and taught from the beginning' (v. 1). Jesus *did things and taught,* and note that the doing came first: he was undoubtedly someone characterised first by doing, then by teaching. This doing is not to be understood moralistically, as we might think, meaning Jesus behaved well and then said all the right and beautiful things. Jesus' powerful, charismatic activity was his healings and miracles. Jesus began to act with power, 'he went about doing good and healing all who were oppressed by the devil' (Acts 10:38), and he taught. So, perhaps we can say that Jesus did not always and solely preach the kerygma but that he also did things, acted, and this was part of his mission.

Finally, we need to add everything the Gospels allow us to understand without stopping to describe it. Except in the case of Luke, most of Jesus' life, that is, a good thirty years of it, is without words, without kerygma. As far as we can tell, Jesus arrives at adulthood without ever having uttered a kerygmatic word. Only some very brief utterances of his are reported. 'Why were you searching for me? Did you not know that I must be in my Father's house?', or the fact that he questioned the teachers.

In conclusion, our answer to the question of whether Jesus preached the kerygma or not is very much nuanced because Jesus' image is not a simple one: he spent a lifetime that is not easy to grasp in a unified way. We need to become disciples of his life, attending to it lovingly and carefully, listening to his explicit preaching and his preaching in parables, his silent preaching and the times when his words were incomprehensible even to the apostles. We think the kerygma should be clear, easy to recall, and we are often led to draw overly simplistic conclusions about how Jesus reveals God, the Father. The Gospels are a warning to us of how much the apostles struggled to understand Jesus and his word, because they were part of a complex way of communication of the divine to humankind.

The parables in Jesus' preaching

We can now offer a first reflection on the place these forms of veiled kerygma known as the parables had in Jesus' preaching. To respond it is useful to divide the material into a number of points:

1. How many parables are there? Exegetes come up with different tallies: it depends on whether or not we consider some very brief stories to be parables. The agreed number is forty two. Some count as many as sixty, but forty two is well-founded, and also includes rather succinct ones, leaving aside simple figures of speech, proverbs, lots of comparisons that would send the number even beyond the higher figure of sixty.

Forty two is already a substantial number (more or less the same as the number of miracles) and they make up a good part of the gospel. Others of Jesus' sermons – the Sermon on the Mount, the one on mission, the eschatological discourse – are part of the Gospels; yet the parables occupy a substantial part too.

How many are there for each evangelist? Six in Mark, twenty two in Matthew, thirty one in Luke. Mark highlights his set; considering that among all of Jesus' sermons, addresses, he reports only the parable type, his six are almost everything Jesus says.

Not all the Synoptics have the same parables. If we regroup the material according to the evangelical tradition, where the triple tradition means Matthew, Mark and Luke, the double tradition Matthew and Luke, and the single tradition means parables or passages found only in Matthew or Luke, we can say that Mark's six parables belong to the triple tradition. In real terms, though, Matthew and Luke only include four of them. But the other two do belong equally to the triple tradition and we can say they have been omitted for some reason.

Of the double tradition, common to Matthew and Luke, there are nine. For the single traditions: Matthew nine and Luke eighteen.

These numbers already indicate that there are few parables of the triple tradition. Given that this tradition responds, more or less, to the primitive outlines of preaching handed down in the communities as basic teaching, we should conclude that effectively, the parables did not play much part in the early preaching of the Christian communities, or so it seems. They were picked up later in the memory of Jesus. This seems to be borne out by the fact that the Acts of the Apostles does not include parables, nor does Paul have any parables, although he employs some analogies, some figures of speech.

So, the parable seems to have a special structure: it emerges in Jesus' life, is less present in the primitive preaching and returns when the community recovers many of his parables while collecting all the Master's sayings.

Clearly, we are in the area of conjecture and can never reach any final conclusion. But we do understand that the parables represent a difficult issue constantly under discussion by exegetes.

To the question about the place they have in Jesus' preaching, we say that he undoubtedly included many parables in his discourses. As for the place they had in the primitive preaching, it is difficult to know.

2. When did Jesus tell the parables? Sometimes it has been said that they were characteristic of his early preaching. This is partly true and partly not, because we have some parables situated in the final moments of his life. For example, the parable of the wicked tenants (Mark 12) is situated at the time Jesus is about to be killed, and there is already strong opposition to him. Also, the parable of the fig tree that Jesus cursed – a very interesting one we will come back to – is situated in the final days of his life. Then, there are a handful of Luke's parables in his central chapters, during the so-called journey from Galilee to Jerusalem, hence mid-way through Jesus' ministry: for example, the parables in Chapter 15 (the prodigal son, the lost sheep, the woman who finds her coin) and the banquet parables in Chapter 14. So, Jesus used parables at the beginning, halfway through and at the end of his preaching. He willingly employed the language of parable at any moment.

In personal meditation, we can ask him: 'What did you want to say? What revelation of the mystery of the Father were you telling us about, or hiding through the parables? And why were you hiding something?'

Here, our conversation can become as intense as Moses': Why, Lord, why?

3. *How were the parables told?* Almost certainly without public explanation. It is true that the Gospels indicate how Jesus explained them to the disciples, but in private. So, they were not a simple teaching ploy like when we offer an example, then say: the example means this, or that. The parables are told in order to unnerve or unsettle the people. Afterwards, the disciples questioned Jesus, but the explanation, e.g. as reported by Matthew 13:18-23, is probably the result of the early community. This indicates that the early community did reflect on the parables, even if we do not know how and when.

4. *What do the parables speak about?* We will see this by analysing them in groups. Nevertheless, there is already an easy answer; for example, in Matthew 13, when speaking about the mustard seed, the yeast, the hidden treasure, the pearl, the net (five parables) he says each time: 'The kingdom of heaven is like ... '. And again, 'For the kingdom of heaven is like a landowner who went out early in the morning to hire labourers for his vineyard' (Mt 20:1).

So, they are often, but not always, parables of the kingdom. Luke's parables are rather in reference to particular situations: in Chapter 15 they are aimed at getting some people to see the error of their ways for criticising Jesus and grumbling because he mixed with sinners. In Chapter 18, the parable of the pharisee and the publican is aimed at people who thought themselves to be righteous.

The term 'parables of the kingdom' is not applied as such in an unambiguous way to all the parables, even though many are clearly able to be classified under that heading.

If we ask ourselves in more detailed fashion how they can be classified by content, a division into four groups (a necessarily schematic one) becomes useful:
- Parables of the seed, or the beginning;
- Parables of the call, invitation, tied especially to banquets;
- Parables of the lost and found, or return;
- Parables of judgement, or the end.

There are four basic themes and we will look at them in the following order: the seed (beginning), the judgement (end); the lost and found (conversion), the call (vocation).

Naturally, it is not possible to fit all the parables into these categories, since some are more nuanced. I am unsure, for example, where to put one of the most important ones, the one about the Good Samaritan. Perhaps it could be seen as a parable of conversion, of invitation ('Go and do likewise').

No distinction can sum up all of the overflowing abundance of Jesus' preaching: avoiding categorisation and following his inner emotion, he tells parables, intervenes, explains comparisons. Perhaps the most important thing we should do is not to analyse any parable too much (this is the exegetes' task) but listen to the heart of Christ speaking.

'Lord, let me enter your heart. What did you have within when you told the parables? What clarifications, what focus, what emotion, what indignation, what cry was urging you to use that language?'

The parables are in no way a gentle teaching: rather they are weapons of war, moments of struggle, cries that arise from deep inner emotion, however veiled and pedagogically well-dispensed they may be. The world of the parable lets us penetrate Jesus' power in communicating the mystery of God, and also his wisdom, attention to the other, his irony, humour and ability to navigate difficult situations without awkwardness and with great elegance. It is a way of understanding the mystery of God in Christ revealed to human beings.

Questioning the Teacher

At this point, we can draw some practical applications, some useful warnings.

1. *Avoid all hasty conclusions,* including in pastoral ministry. Reading books or articles here and there on the parables, sometimes I find myself faced with hasty conclusions. For example, some say that the parable is the ordinary way of catechising because Jesus always spoke in parables. It is not really true that Jesus only spoke in parables. Or there are some who arrive at the opposite conclusion: Jesus spoke openly about the kingdom of God, and we can do no other than proclaim the kerygma in all its absoluteness. That is not true! Jesus preached the kerygma openly and also preached it in veiled form.

Overly condensed views of the gospel are always risky. Sometimes even our pastoral activity, when done in haste, suffers from this kind of superficiality: we take a phrase, one of Jesus' ways of acting, and translate it into our own way of acting, drawing conclusions from it; yet, someone else with a good sense of everyday life sees that things are not going so well. We are called to contemplate Jesus, not to formulate hasty summaries.

2. *Listen and be patient:* there is need for a lot of listening and a lot of patience to arrive at that knowledge of God promised to whoever truly follows Jesus in evangelical life. We listen and are patient, because the Lord is merciful, beyond us, and one gets to know him only through experience and prayer.

It is a truth we will never sufficiently learn; often we are impatient, in a hurry, even in the desire to know God and his plan for us. Or we get upset if we do not succeed in seeing things clearly straight away: 'Why is this, or something else happening?' 'What is it trying to tell me?' And we head off in some weird direction, including at the spiritual or pastoral level, or make life choices by drawing hasty conclusions from a single event, a single word. Listening and patience, then, in order to get to know the Lord.

The African world, on the other hand – or so it seems to me – is a world of great patience, a world that teaches us to put aside haste. Martha was hasty, and Jesus praises Mary who was patient, listening, letting time pass, and not immediately asking what she must do. She is somewhat symbolic of the Oriental world, while Martha is of the West, where we are always concerned about acting, doing, doing in a hurry, seeing everything clearly. The exercise of listening is necessary to recover the sense of God who does not reveal himself against our will but out of love, in gentleness, silence, in Elijah's 'breeze'. God reveals himself in the gentle winds of patience and a humble heart.

3. *Question the Teacher*, speak with Jesus: 'Lord, why did you tell this parable? Why did you express yourself this way? Why did you not speak more clearly in certain situations? Why did you accept that the people might not understand what you were saying? Why did you not reveal yourself, given the darkness the people were immersed in? Lord, what is your way of revealing the Father? How was the fire that you wanted to bring to this earth, burning in your heart?'

It is of huge benefit to question your inner Teacher in peace and patience, with the certainty that he has the answers and will pass them on to you at the right time, without hiding anything, because he is the Truth. More than answers, it is humble dialogue that is important wherein I speak trustfully with the Lord amid the contradictions of life and ask him to nurture me at the 'opportune time.' St Augustine teaches us that conversing with the Teacher is already to enter eternal life, already to be on top of every specific problem, because it is equivalent to possessing the truth in love. If we do not yet have an answer to this doubt, that concern, that worrying situation, having it already as part of this humble adoration of the Teacher is already being in love and truth, already beginning the dialogue that will never end. This is why Jesus can say: 'Mary has chosen the better part *which will not be taken away from her!*'

At a certain point, Jesus will sit down at the table and Mary's listening will finish: '... will not be taken away from her' means, then, the ongoing dialogue which, more than everything else, is communication in the Father with Christ. With this a mysterious light shines, sometimes masked, but sufficient for finding our way through the problems of life in serenity and peace.

This is one teaching of the parables; a blinding light is not always needed; the Lord can reveal himself in mystery, in hiddenness. In fact, we will see that the main parables are the ones about the hidden seed, the hidden yeast, the tiny mustard seed, all invisible. The parables thus allow us to enter the mystery of God, which is closed to the petulance and pretence of those who would like to clarify the mystery for their own use and consumption. This is true for so many circumstances: it is true in life, in sickness, in death, true for all the events of life where we want to know 'why'; but often our 'why' is satisfied only when it is transformed through adoration and humble dialogue about ourselves, others, what happens in the Church.

It is by questioning the Teacher that we enter into the true kerygma of Jesus, who is precisely this way of revealing the Father.

Let us call on Mary of Bethany to help us listen to the Word of God patiently and without haste.

> 'Lord,
> through the intercession of Mary of Bethany
> may I also come to know you as Teacher,
> as the *didaskalos,*
> that is, with your ability to teach,
> act, live and love.'

PARABLES OF THE SEED

'Lord, we follow you
step by step,
without clearly knowing where you want to take us.
We trust in your word,
and we trust that on the mountain you will show
    yourself,
as you showed yourself on the mountain
to Peter, James and John;
as you showed yourself on the mountain to Moses; as
    you showed yourself on Mount Calvary.
Grant us the grace and perseverance to climb,
step by step, up the mountain
without tiring,
taking each step in the certainty
that it is drawn by your love, by your truth.
Grant perseverance to our steps,
may we not be distracted,
nor sit down lazily,
but carry out every moment of our day
with the certainty of being led,
conducted and attracted by your truth
and your mercy.
Forgive us, Lord,
if somewhere along the way we stumble,

fall or draw aside.
Give us relief and breath as we walk
toward the mount of contemplation.'

In walking toward the mount of contemplation, let us now allow ourselves to be enlightened by the first group of parables – those of the seed or the beginning, because the seed is a beginning. We shall ask ourselves which and how many are these parables, what are they saying, and we will try to understand who Jesus was telling them to and what was in his heart as he spoke.

The five parables of the seed: a *lectio* of Mark 4:1-9

1. *There are three basic parables of the seed* recorded by Mark in Chapter 4: the sower, the seed that grows of its own accord, the mustard seed. The first and third are common to the other two Synoptics, only Mark has the second. To these I would add, for reasons of their affinity, the *parable of the yeast (also a hidden beginning of a seed-like nature)* common to Matthew (3:33) and Luke (13:20), and the *parable of the weeds and the good seed* (Mt 13:36-40). This last named is very similar in its first part to the parable of the sower: the seed is cast and then an opposite force – the devil, the cares of life, riches, persecutions – steal it and choke it. Nevertheless, the parable of the weeds also belongs to the parables of 'the end' because it insists on the last judgement: in the end, the weeds will be burnt and the angels will reap the good crop.

As we have already said, it is not easy to clearly classify the parables. We would like to consider these five as a group because of their affinity in context, pedagogy, teaching. They all have something small, humble, hidden about them which, despite the difficulties and the opposition they experience, bears fruit, becomes visible and grows. The underlying idea does not yet express the power of the parables but it does help us understand the process of thought that makes it possible to look at them together.

2. *What do the five parables of the seed say?* To respond, it is necessary to read them carefully. The way the account is structured also helps us grasp the teaching. The best thing to do is to do a *lectio,* seeking to understand the supporting elements, and then a brief *meditatio*. I will entrust four of the parables to your personal work and together we will spend time on just one, the first, which is the fundamental one because Jesus tells his disciples: 'Do you not understand this parable? Then how will you understand all the parables?' (Mk 4:13). So it is somewhat of a gateway, the key to understanding the others or, at least, the necessary route. This is also why it is a parable of beginnings.

A lectio of Mark 4:1-9

> Again, he began to teach beside the sea. Such a very large crowd gathered around him that he got into a boat on the sea and sat there, while the whole crowd was beside the sea on the land. He began to teach them many things in parables and in his teaching he said to them ... (vv. 1-2).

What emerges as we re-read the first two verses? That certain words appear three times. Firstly, the word 'teach': 'he began to *teach*'; 'he *began to teach ... in parables*'; 'in his *teaching* he said to them.' We know that when a word in Scripture is repeated three times it means it is important.

Another repeated word is the *sea* ('*thalassa*'). 'He began to teach beside *the sea*'; 'he got into a boat *on the sea*'; 'the crowd was *beside the sea*.'

Teaching indicates that Jesus was acting as a rabbi, as a teacher, because he wanted to communicate something, wanted them to go on a journey of understanding. The parables, then, are part of his living magisterium, his teaching. When we hear the word *teacher* we understand it in a school context, but here Jesus is a teacher of life, a teacher with the prophetic power of warning, reproof, anger. The parable comes out of his being a teacher who is concerned about the people undertaking a certain journey, including a mental one.

'Lord, help me to take this journey you wanted taken with your parables. Tell me what you wanted to say.'

The sea. Why so much insistence on the sea? Was it because Mark, a very succinct writer, wanted to highlight the word? We note that 'Again he began to teach' indicates a reference to earlier circumstances. The one immediately preceding is the mountain: 'He went up the mountain and called to him those whom he wanted ... and he appointed twelve' (Mk 3:14). In a previous verse, before the mountain was the sea once again: 'Jesus departed with his disciples to the sea, and a great multitude from Galilee followed him; hearing all that he was doing, they came to him in great numbers from Judea, Jerusalem, Idumea, beyond the Jordan, and the region around Tyre and Sidon' (3:7-8).

The expression 'Again he began to teach,' with which Mark begins our parable refers, then, to the first time: Jesus taught in the synagogue, then 'departed' to the sea almost to be alone. The people reached him there; from there he went up the mountain and from the mountain returned to the sea.

The visual image is insisted on so much for a symbolic reason that it perhaps escapes us. We need to enter into the mentality of the Jews to understand the value symbols held for them – how symbols alluded to the history of salvation when they came from an expert rabbi who knew the language of Scripture. Certainly here, in the teaching of Jesus at the seaside, even his being seated 'on' the sea has great symbolic import. While the mountain is the place of God's presence – Jesus chooses his Twelve on the mountain – the sea is the Red Sea, the place of turbulent human events, a place of danger, risk, confusion, instability. Jesus comes to be with human instability, human fragility, there where the crowd of sick, miserable people are who do not even know what they want. He comes to the poor, the most desperate. Jesus even goes *onto the sea* – the Israelite memory would go back to the power of God who divided the Red Sea, brought order to the primitive chaos of the waters, who divided the waters of earth. The one who is recounting this story thus reads into it the power of Jesus over the tribulations and disorders of daily existence.

'Whoever reads things this way is already contemplating you, Lord, master of the seas, master of all the many tribulations of the human race. Lord, you sit yourself down amid the mysterious ways of history and we entrust ourselves to you, sit near you to hear those words that can enlighten our way along the dark roads and the often impenetrable paths in the forest of human events.'

'Listen! A sower went out to sow. And as he sowed, some seed fell on the path and the birds came and ate it up. Other seed fell on rocky ground, where it did not have much soil, and it sprang up quickly, since it had no depth of soil. And when the sun rose, it was scorched; and since it had no root, it withered away. Other seed fell among thorns, and the thorns grew up and choked it, and it yielded no grain. Other seed fell into good soil and brought forth grain, growing up and increasing and yielding thirty and sixty and a hundredfold.' And he said, 'Let anyone with ears to hear listen!' (Mk 4:3-9)

This is the parable in its enigmatic, mysterious form. Meanwhile, I am struck by how the parable is framed by a double invitation to listen; it begins by saying 'Listen!' and ends with the words 'Let anyone with ears to hear listen.' Jesus the teacher is saying, 'Pay attention!' This is not just a superfluous expression like we sometimes say. Jesus wants to advise them: 'I am about to say something that closely concerns you but you will need to use your intelligence.'

We are invited to use our intelligence not only for listening as a physical act. In fact, he will later complain: 'They listen and do not hear, look and do not see.' Jesus asks for intelligent listening, a listening that asks itself: 'What is behind this? What does he want to say? How does it concern or touch me?' So, a characteristic of parable is that it is about *involvement*: these are words relevant *to me*, they concern *me*, they are about *me*.

Again, there is a word recurring three times: *sow*. 'A *sower* went out to *sow*. And as he *sowed*, some seed fell ...' The theme of sower and seed is stressed. These images of agrarian life are not to be thought of as accidental, because through them the mysteries of the kingdom find expression. It harks back to the mindset of Psalm 126: 'Those who go out weeping, bear the seed for sowing' (v. 5). To sow means to entrust a life to its vital journey, to begin a vital process with trust. The metaphor is very dear to Jesus and to all of Scripture because it is descriptive of the Word, of faith in one's personal journey. We will come back to these images of the natural kingdom. It is enough to say here that Jesus reads the mysteries of the kingdom in them with profound intelligence.

Let us briefly look at the four growth situations.

The first is dealt with quickly: something falls on the path, the birds come and eat it.

The second is expressed in three lines and is more developed compared to the first. There is the rocky ground and the concept is repeated three times: there was not much soil, it was not very deep, there were no roots. The situation is presented for its fragility. Soil, roots, depth are extremely allusive terms in biblical language. However, even in this second situation, while there is a little bit of growth it ends up as nothing, scorched.

The third: 'Other seed fell among thorns and the thorns grew up and choked it and it yielded no grain.' It does not say it didn't grow. In the second case, it was scorched after germination. Here the seed grew but did not yield grain. It germinated but there was no bearing of fruit which is the ultimate aim of growth. We can recall similar images: the fig in leaf that bore no fruit; the vineyard of Israel that produced sour grapes.

The fourth situation is expressed solemnly, with a broader correspondence of words in the image of the good soil. The fullness is described carefully: 'Other seed fell into good soil and brought forth grain' [here it is the seed, more than the grain], 'growing up and increasing and yielding... .' It is interesting that in the Greek text, while the three categories are in the singular – one falls on the path, another on the rocks, another in thorns – now it says 'others' in the plural. It is the plurality of seeds that fall on good soil, and then [the Greek text] strangely returns to the singular, speaking of the growth of all these seeds: 'And it yielded one thirty, another sixty and another a hundredfold.'

The four situations are in a literary crescendo, building up images and attention to detail.

This brief *lectio* will also help your personal reading of the other four parables. Now we will consider some starting points for a *meditatio* by asking some questions.

Starting points for *meditatio*

Where does the emphasis of the parable fall? It is very important to grasp this. In fact, if the account were to stop at the first, second or third image, the emphasis would be on the sad fate of the seed. On Jesus' part, it would have been a warning not to waste the Word of God, not to mistreat it.

Instead, the parable goes to the fourth stage. Jesus' intention is certainly to put people on guard (otherwise he would only have told the last part); however, it is more complex, with many elements. The emphasis falls on the final result and with a special detail. Even though I am no expert in agriculture, it seems to me that ordinarily a seed will not produce a hundredfold, not even in the best of cases. There is an exaggeration in the parable and where there is exaggeration that is where the central point will be, what the parable hinges on.

Leaving it to your meditation to explore many other ideas, I will try to express what the parable is trying to say. The seed is *sown*, entrusted to its vital course of human freedom; *with trust* because the one who is sowing it somehow leaves it to its fate; and with *great tolerance*, allowing it freedom, not staying to see where he has sown, to the extent that some seed falls outside the field; the seed is *hidden* and can barely be seen at the beginning; it meets adversity, opposition and difficulties, but despite a few defeats it is *victorious*, a hundredfold is an extraordinary way of growing.

These are some of the key elements that help us grasp what the parable is saying. We will not be looking for the application here; it is better to dwell on the parable itself. I would prefer to develop the importance of the metaphors of the farming world as we find them in the New Testament.

The theme of the sower, for example, returns in St Paul's agricultural image: 'I planted, Apollos watered, but God gave the growth. So, neither the one who plants nor the one who waters is anything, but only God who gives the growth' (1 Cor 3:5-7).

The theme of the roots recurs in Ephesians 3:17 among others: 'as you are being rooted and grounded in love,' having one's roots in charity.

The theme of bearing fruit expresses the attractive fullness of Christian life, the fruits of the spirit (love, kindness, joy, peace). They are all images taken up and further explored in the New Testament. Yet it can be helpful to clear up a misunderstanding. In the modern interpretation of the parables, starting from Jülicher, then Jeremias, and up to contemporary commentators, the insistence is that the power of the parables does not lie in allegory, that is, in taking individual words and transporting them, but in a single, central idea usually expressed in the parable's climactic moment. If, on the one hand, it is true that the central idea is important, on the other we should not claim that the parable has no metaphorical energy, or that there is no capacity within the community to develop metaphorical language!

Because it has in fact done so. The power of the parable is also that it encourages a taste for metaphor. Metaphor has deep roots (as we will see) because there is a parallel between the journey of faith and the journey of life in the world. There is a certain mysterious harmony which Jesus teaches us to discover and which, besides, the human being already instinctively discovers. Faith has its own development, and the human being can find some analogies in the journey of life, like the journey of the seed, for understanding the mystery of faith. Jesus experienced all this very intensely; the early community experienced it, the Fathers of the Church experienced it – they applied the parables, at times exaggeratedly, to different historical situations. This is not alien to Jesus' way of thinking and his metaphorical language, so long as we keep intact the fundamental essence of the parable.

It would be wonderful to be able to continue this reflection by thinking how true the comparison is between the seed and the beginning of the life of the Word in the heart. The seed comes from on high, not from the ground, and the Word of God comes from outside us; it is not the spontaneous product of religious indwelling, but once it has entered this terrain, the Word too, like the seed, becomes one with the earth; it does not remain something outside. Beginning from the earth, from its insertion at the heart of life, it slowly buds with barely visible beginnings. Sometimes we would like to immediately see results in conversions: instead we need to content ourselves with watching the slow beginnings. Then, with the eyes of faith and despite seeing little, we should perceive that development is taking place and that we need to defend this tender little shoot from rocks, thorns, all the forces lined up against it. Pastoral activity does not create the seed: that comes from God, but the response is human, from the earth. The pastor is the one who carefully discerns the seed, patiently removes what is hindering it and encourages what fosters its growth. The pastor does not own this seed, just as he is not the one who makes it grow (because that is God alone). He cannot enforce freedom, only facilitate God's action. It is not up to us to provoke the favourable response that comes from freedom, given that even God entrusts himself to human freedom, that is, to the province of the heart, even accepting setbacks and negative responses.

We can derive an insightful reflection from these agricultural images, then, about what we often mean in generic terms by pastoral activity or 'God's farming'. 'Look at the birds of the air, consider the lilies of the field'; try to understand the life of these beings and then you will better understand similarly, how the life of the spirit is first of all almost invisible, then sprouts and develops.

The audience: those who heard the parables

What kind of people are in the presence of the speaker? Let me suggest some answers to this.

1. The person speaking is facing an audience, I believe, which he needs to work at in order to capture their interest. That also happens to us when we preach: we note that the public is not attentive, is somewhat tired, distracted and to wake them up we tell a story.

Jesus is facing an audience he needs to shake up; he has to get them involved, try to get them to imagine the circumstances of the fragile, almost invisible but powerful seed.

2. However, he must respect the particular limitations of his audience. If this were not so, he would speak more clearly. It is not easy to guess what these limitations were: perhaps they were not willing to listen; an audience that needed to be led on very slowly, because they could not see deeper connections. There is a need to start from things that are fairly evident, things the audience can recognise, then get them to move on from there. Perhaps there are political or sociological misunderstandings, suspicions surrounding Jesus' words. He knows he is suspect because already in Chapter 3 of Mark he was accused of being Satan! He needs to be aware of this situation: suspicion, manipulation, political factionalism ('he is for us; against us…'). So Jesus uses language that disturbs them all to some extent because it cannot easily be categorised as coming from this or that group, from right or left, for or against the Romans, Herod.

It is confusing language but it goes to the heart.

3. It is probably an audience that could reject a direct approach: so an audience not only less disposed but positively ill-disposed.

We can conclude by saying that the parables of the seed (the same thing goes for the other four) are the kerygma offered to a difficult people. Therefore, they are a real act of teaching (Jesus is the Teacher, Rabbi) but also an act of courtesy, respect for freedom, an act of adaptation to their level, an act of tenderness, mercy. It is attentiveness to the fragility of individuals that allows us to appreciate how kind is Jesus the Teacher, how patient is Jesus the Rabbi, and how he is in no hurry. Someone in a hurry spills it all out immediately. Instead, Jesus accepts that it takes time for the people to understand, that some are questioning; what is most important for him right now is to encourage questions that open the heart to fresh questions and insights and not to say everything at once.

We need to admit that we do not always imitate his patience. Sometimes, the impatience of 'everything at once' is necessary, while at other times it does not correspond to the gradual development of the seed and hence to human freedom.

Jesus' heart

What is *within* the person speaking? What is in you, Jesus, while you are speaking this way?

1. The person speaking in this way has a strong *emotional component* within, a burning desire to communicate. Speaking in parables is not a question of refined metaphorical technique but a need to say something very serious or urgent yet adapt it to the limitations of the situation. The parable comes spontaneously when there is such an inner urge that it reveals itself, even in difficult circumstances of suspicion, debate, manipulation. In his heart, Jesus has the mystery of the kingdom, the need to communicate the mystery of the Father, and he does it by speaking in parables.

2. The person speaking thus has a *very sure message, one fully integrated with who he is*. He is as sure as the water

flowing down the mountainside. When it finds a rock it goes around, below, over, but flows ever onward. The clarity of the message is like crystal clear water in a flood that goes around all obstacles in its course. Where the message cannot be expressed directly, it is expressed differently. This is why Jesus tells many parables, not just one: 'the kingdom of God is like…. is like…. is like…'

With the kingdom in his heart, he has no difficulty finding the best method of expression that is appropriate to his listeners in their circumstances. Jesus creates the parable, driven by the sure power of the message that urges him on in his heart. We do not know how to create parables when our message is weak, tied to memory (we need to consult the book; need to question the catechesis; need to look at this; review that): when it does not come from within us and is something badly learned that comes unstuck.

3. The person speaking thus has *a great sense of the indefinability of the mystery*. The mystery of God is so deep that it can be formulated in very many ways. Jesus is not afraid of telling the strangest, freshest parables that all say the same thing in many different ways; and still not everything has been said. In his heart, there is the awareness that the mystery is of the beyond and only comparisons, examples, metaphors can be used to point to it. We note that he never says *what it is* and he does not say so because it is indefinable: he says 'it is like a man…. It is like a field…it is like a net.'

4. The person speaking thus has *a great sense of the economy of the mystery of God*, of the fatherly, gradual, deferential distribution with which God dispenses the grain of the Word. He does not throw the Word in our face but disseminates it

with a sense of the economy of the mystery of God, in the Greek sense of '*dispensatio*', or respect for freedom, a deep awareness of the human heart and its tortuous and difficult paths. It involves great patience and kindness. The sense of the economy of the mystery of God finds typical expression in the New Testament in the Letter to the Philippians (4:5): '*to epieikés*', moderation, a sense of the individual's convenience, a sense of situation and place; not out of fearful prudence but because the mystery of God, with its times and approaches, is great. This is why Jesus can act with the greatest freedom.

'Lord,
what is there when I speak about God?
Is it your strong urge to communicate,
your very sure message,
the sense of indefinability of the mystery of God?
Lord and Teacher,
teach me to speak in parables.'

THE POWER OF THE PARABLES OF THE SEED

Continuing with our theme, we would like to try to understand the specific power of the parables.

In the New Testament, especially in the Letters of St Paul, the power of the gospel proclamation is connected with the freedom and openness of its proclamation. The Greek word *'parresia'* is in fact used to indicate the frankness, freedom, courage of the Word. In this regard, it is interesting to reread at least some lines from the Second Letter to the Corinthians:

> Such is the confidence that [*as apostles and proclaimers of the gospel*] we have through Christ towards God. Not that we are competent of ourselves to claim anything as coming from us; our competence is from God, who has made us competent to be ministers of a new covenant… Since, then, we have such a hope, we act *with great boldness*.… (3:4–6,12).

> Therefore, since it is by God's mercy that we are engaged in this ministry, we do not lose heart. We have renounced the shameful things that one hides; we refuse to practise cunning or to falsify God's word; *but by the open statement of truth* we commend ourselves to the conscience of everyone in the sight of God (4:1-2).

Let us ask ourselves how this power, this frankness, freedom and openness is found in the parables which are, by nature, a mysterious, enigmatic, hidden kind of language, a questioning and developing kind of language, meaning it only gradually reveals the truth.

I suggest the following points for our reflection:
- What is the linguistic, literary, verbal force or power of the parable?
- What is the power of the parables of the seed?
- Where am I when faced with the power of the kingdom?
- Finally, a brief practical application on a particular examination of conscience.

The specific power of parable

We begin with two parables from outside our present context. They are very effective because they refer to particular, well-defined cases with all circumstances specified. They will help us gain a better grasp of the power of parables.

1. First of all, the parable that *Nathan told David* to convince him of his sin. We find it in 2 Samuel 12, preceded by Chapter 11 containing some of the richest pages of psychology and truth in the Old Testament. A devout and good king who loves God deeply and is most attentive to his friends rapidly becomes an adulterer and a killer, step by step; the victim is his best friend. Daily experience confirms the truth of this passage – the ease with which David sins and with which a person can end up killing a friend by beginning with small mistakes and pretexts.

Chapter 12 presumes the facts of this sin:

> ..... and the LORD sent Nathan to David. He came to him and said to him, 'There were two men in a certain city, the one rich and the other poor. The rich man had very many flocks and herds; but the poor man had nothing but one little ewe lamb which he had bought. He brought it up and it grew up with him and his children; it used to eat of meagre fare, and drink from his cup, and lie in his bosom, and it was like a daughter to him. Now there came a traveller to the rich man, and he was loath to take one of his own flock or herd to prepare for the wayfarer who had come to him, but he took the poor man's lamb and prepared that for the guest who had come to him.' Then David's anger was greatly kindled against the man. He said to Nathan, 'As the LORD lives, the man who has done this deserves to die; he shall restore the lamb fourfold, because he did this thing and because he had no pity.' Nathan said to David, 'You are the man! Thus, says the LORD, the God of Israel: I anointed you king over Israel, and I rescued you from the hand of Saul; I gave you your master's house and your master's wives into your bosom, and gave you the house of Israel and of Judah, and if that had been too little, I would have added as much more. Why have you despised the word of the LORD, to do what is evil in his sight? You have struck down Uriah the Hittite with the sword and have taken his wife to be your wife, and have killed him with the sword of the Ammonites (2 Sam 12:1-9).

The power of the parable here is very clear. What is the situation? It is that of a great and powerful man who has committed a great injustice, has done great evil and is probably being gossiped about. As always happens, people talk about it and gossip, but no one dares tell him the truth, no one dares speak directly to him. Everyone clams up as soon as David approaches, and when he sends his courtiers away, they begin complaining again. The king is destined to remain a slave to his sin because no one will help him.

The problem, therefore, is how to help David. The best thing would be to go to him and tell him he has done wrong. Perhaps Nathan did not lack courage, like many other prophets did not lack it in similar situations; nevertheless, we need to consider that David would not be well-disposed to accepting a direct warning. There is no sin so great that a human being cannot find a reason to justify it. 'Basically,' David would have said, 'Bathsheba wasn't getting on with Uriah; he treated her badly and I gave him a hand; perhaps Uriah would have betrayed me one day, so I did to him what he would have done to me.' Perhaps David had settled for a whole series of justifications. Besides, like any monarch, if someone accused him, he would have become suspicious. 'They are against me, perhaps there is a plot. I need to do something!' The situation, then, is difficult, and a direct challenge would not have worked. What does Nathan do? He tries to involve David by getting him to make a judgement, whereby David sides with what is right, because he is a man who wants to defend the weak. Taken by this positive side of things, at a certain point, he is caught in the trap: now the object of his judgement is himself.

2. The other parable is in Luke's Gospel, Chapter 7. *Simon* has welcomed Jesus into his house and suddenly a *woman*

of ill-repute comes in, throws herself at Jesus' feet, pours out fragrant oil, washes his feet with her tears and dries them with her hair, then kisses them and anoints them with the oil.

> Now, when the Pharisee who had invited him saw it, he said to himself, 'If this man were a prophet, he would have known who and what kind of woman this is who is touching him – that she is a sinner.' Jesus spoke up and said to him, 'Simon, I have something to say to you.' 'Teacher,' he replied, 'Speak.' 'A certain creditor had two debtors; one owed five hundred denarii, and the other fifty. When they could not pay, he cancelled the debts for both of them. Now which of them will love him more?' Simon answered, 'I suppose the one for whom he cancelled the greater debt.' And Jesus said to him, 'You have judged rightly.' Then turning toward the woman, he said To Simon, 'Do you see this woman? I entered your house; you gave me no water for my feet, but she has bathed my feet with her tears and dried them with her hair. You gave me no kiss, but from the time I came in she has not stopped kissing my feet. You did not anoint my head with oil but she has anointed my feet with ointment. Therefore, I tell you, her sins, which were many, have been forgiven; hence, she has shown great love. But the one to whom little is forgiven, loves little (vv. 39-47).

Here, too, the power of the parable is clear. It has suddenly involved Simon, despite himself, and he has nothing to say because he is the one who made the judgement.

What is the situation? Simon is a presumptuous man and perhaps he thinks he has earned worth of some kind for the invitation he extended to Jesus. He is not very courteous, has not wanted to put himself out too much, and is looking to be well regarded. He is a difficult man and jumps to conclusions, because when he sees the woman he judges her from his exalted position.

How to lovingly get him to understand his error? Hence, the words of wisdom with which Jesus gradually catches him in a judgement that seems right: only after having passed judgement does Simon see that he has become part of it. Jesus' words are quite strong and remind us of Nathan's 'You are that man!' All the power of the kerygma explodes after Simon has been prepared and becomes involved. Like the power of Nathan's indignation, it acts through the roundabout layers of the parable. Jesus' disappointment at what is happening, there from the beginning, is expressed through the perceptive, and elegant power of the *'mashál'* (the allegory) to involve Simon and directly admonish him.

Not all parables have the same characteristics, but these two, being told to specific individuals and for precise situations, enable us to see more easily the specific power they have. It is not just a case of a simple little teaching device, not even an 'audio visual' from the ancient church: it is a strong word, cast in wisdom form, to prepare for the truth it already contains.

It seems to me that the power of parable has four features:

> – *Involvement*: the parable turns the listeners into an actor in the story, incorporates them by asking for a judgement: 'Whoever has ears to hear, listen': try to understand, enter into it and you will understand.

– *The seriousness of the situation*: the parable is not about an abstract theory but a real, existential situation. David has sinned gravely, his reputation is at risk, his credibility is crumbling, we need to help him. Simon is presumptuous, jumps to conclusions, despises the woman, while the truth of the gospel demands clarity and understanding. On the other hand, clarifying the situation is difficult.

– *Reversal*: things are reversed. David judges and is judged; Simon, a pretentious and boorish host, is shown up for what he is. The one who thinks he is superior is brought low and vice versa. The woman who is the sinner is held up as a model of faith and love. The power of the parable is disconcerting.

– *Focus*: the parable has a wealth of elements to it; at a certain point it comes to a 'climax', something its power hinges on. In 2 Samuel 12, this climax is Nathan's words: 'You are the man!' and the whole conversation depends on it. The various elements become focused and take on the power of a battering ram demolishing its target through involvement rather than by direct blow.

These are four features which help us a little to understand why Jesus spoke in parables.

Parables of the seed: urgency and involvement

What is the power of the parables of the seed? We have tried to say it in the preceding meditation, indirectly, asking ourselves what there is in Jesus who told them and what there was in the people who resisted. Now we want to identify their intrinsic power; it is not easy because it risks exhausting them.

1. First, *the serious situation* that underlies the parables and is the root of their power. I would express it in three sentences: the kingdom exists; the kingdom is unstoppable; the kingdom is here. *This is the power. There is a kingdom and it is in Jesus.* The kingdom is irresistible and no one can stop it. The kingdom is here, now. This is the climax or 'point' of the parables.

Perhaps we find one of the clearest translations of such seriousness in the catechetical, affirmative, descriptive language in Luke 17:20-21:

> Once Jesus was asked by the Pharisees when the kingdom of God was coming, and he answered, 'The kingdom of God is not coming with things that can be observed; nor will they say, "Look, here it is!" or "There it is!" For in fact the kingdom of God is among you.'

These words express all the inner energy of Jesus, who feels he is the kingdom, knows that the kingdom is there and wants to tell of it in many ways, wants to shout it out, but finds himself faced with a confused and unclear situation.

2. *A situation in need of clarification.* The people do not want to open their eyes, are always expecting something showy and sensational. We could say that the spark that ignites the parable comes from the power of proclamation and the counter force of resistance. The people see something

sensational and ask: where is the kingdom of God? Today, too, at least in Europe, people easily flock to a place where there is talk of an apparition, a revelation; they probably need things they can see, sensational things; they struggle to accept that the kingdom is found in simple, little, daily, insignificant things. Jesus comes as if to conceal himself in the depths of the earth and the people ask: where is this seed? Where is this kingdom?

So, it is urgent to open their eyes and understand that the *kingdom is here* despite not having the show and enormous power we imagine the mystery of God to have.

Already we can glimpse the scandal of the cross: the people who struggle to understand the little seed, will have even greater difficulty accepting that the kingdom comes through the cross! God takes flesh in the humility of the Son and in the simplicity of daily life. It is true that Jesus accomplishes some 'signs', the miracles; but what are the miracles? Healing poor people, the lame, the sick. This is not enough.

They want something else.

The power of the parables of the seed, then, could consist of this: it is urgent to grasp what does not appear but in fact exists. The kingdom is here, develops like the little seed, and nothing can stop it. It will find extraordinary success, a hundredfold, unless we reject or resist it. Jesus wants to shout out that the kingdom is here, and they need to believe in the gospel, accept it in faith: 'Believe in the gospel, the kingdom of God is near.'

All this is repeated in our Christian experience. Sometimes we ask ourselves: when will the Lord ever transform me? When will he give me this gift? When will I feel it is a part of my life? When? *Now*. The kingdom of God is here and, if you look for it outside, you will not find it, because it is in faith that salvation will be given you, and you must not be expecting anything else.

Another way of expressing the seriousness of the situation is this: you risk losing what is essential while waiting for something secondary. Whoever welcomes the kingdom in faith already possesses it, because faith is the source of holiness, freedom, righteousness, love, forgiveness.

In the parables of the seed, Jesus takes aim at the laziness, indolence, sensuality of the people who cannot lower themselves to believe, who do not accept small, simple signs, who only allow themselves to be convinced by the power of an army, by money and success, while instead, Jesus presents himself in the humble image of a man, a companion.

Finally, along with urgency, the power of the parable seeks to express involvement: you are this soil; the seed is there and you are the stones or thorns. You who judge and listen to these parables, try to understand what they are saying about you. 'You who have ears to hear, listen.'

Parable and me

Let each one now make a self-examination and look at the seriousness of their situation.

1. An examination on what there is in myself of David, Simon, on *what is in me that resists the clarity of God's word*. Are there sinful situations in me, sometimes serious sin, a life, perhaps, that never succeeds in being clear to itself, and is defensive? Is it sometimes a case of things that should not be and that we never dare to deal with; perhaps things others gossip about and which we legitimise? We 'waterproof' ourselves against these things, not seeing that they compromise our very apostolic effectiveness.

In other cases, they are perhaps simple habits, where we block others out, close ourselves off to them; or it could be relationships we have permanently destroyed. We are not aware of it, but in reality, they are a source of unease for us, an irritant, like sand in the engine of a car. Others could help us, because generally, others have a less emotional judgement than we do. It is in this sense that it could be useful to know what others are saying about us. Mutterings among the people of God can also have some advantage: if we pay attention, we might become aware of things that no one dare tell us! This does not mean we have to please everyone, but it does suggest an insistent prayer to address to God: 'Lord, reveal me to myself; show me the points, places where I struggle to get involved, the things I read or hear that pass me by without touching me. Lord, I know how to tell others beautiful things, important things. I know how to explain them, then I avoid getting involved. Teach me how to apply the parable to myself.'

A first examination, then, can include my asking: what are my inappropriate situations, defensive moments, matters about which I will brook no discussion or criticism?

2. *An examination of my situation.* What makes my current situation serious? Serious in terms of the kingdom of God? What makes it unclear or difficult, in need of clarification?

Probably this seriousness concerns especially the gift of ourselves to God in our daily, patient tasks, without dreaming up other situations. It is about getting the best out of people, or the places we find ourselves in. We struggle to accept these things. The words of Scripture and of Jesus' life can help us a lot. It is not so much the reflection on ourselves that makes us aware of the darkness in us, but reflection on Jesus' life, his words. Only thus can we begin to recognise things: this is for me, this touches me. I can find myself in these words of the psalm, of the gospel, in this attitude of Jesus.

Particular examination

Finally, I would like to offer a practical note on what is called the *particular examination*, and which is less understood today in contrast with a previous era. This particular examination means that in our spiritual planning we constantly fix on one point, no matter how small, focus our attention on it. It is a practice that refers to the principle of focus that we spoke about regarding the parables. A drill is meant to drill down but all its force is focused on one point; similarly, through pedagogical focus on one nerve point of our life, small as it may be, we sometimes achieve notable results with all the rest.

The particular examination, then, is very useful, possibly just because it is all about a specific point. For some, for example, it will consist of clearly determining the time to go to bed or to get up. This may include the need to arrange our day by establishing a timetable, but we keep putting it off. I should do it, but right now it is impossible, there's work to complete, that situation prevents me from establishing fixed times; I will do it when things calm down. And we go on like this for years without really deciding on a point that we know others depend on.

The practice of the particular examination is also valid for our pastoral work. Often, and rightly so, we want to do many things, and it is true that we are asked to do many of them. But if, depending on the various situations, we were to propose diligently carrying out just one aspect of our pastoral role (it could be a point of liturgy, some way of approaching the people or a detail of the Sacrament of Penance), we would gain clarity and facility in many other aspects. Instead, by just tackling a bit here and a bit there, we do not get what we want, and continue to complain that we are swamped by things and that nothing can be done well. We need to convince ourselves that there is always at least one thing that can be done more carefully, and this way, all the others will acquire greater clarity and simplicity.

It is a suggestion we can draw from the fourth feature of the power of parables.

THE PARABLES OF JUDGEMENT

'Holy Spirit,
fill the hearts of your faithful
and kindle in us the same fire
that burned in Jesus' heart
while he spoke of the kingdom of God.
May this fire be passed on to us
as it was given to the disciples of Emmaus.
Grant that we not allow ourselves so much to be overwhelmed,
agitated by the multitude of words,
but that we search behind them
for the fire that is communicated
and inflames our hearts;
only you, Holy Spirit,
can rekindle it,
so to you we turn in our weakness,
in our poverty and with weary hearts,
so that you can rekindle them with warmth,
with holiness of life, the power of the kingdom.'

Today and part of tomorrow are well suited for our time of penance and reconciliation. We have already brought together some points for examination and self-reflection through contemplation of the parables of the seed. What will help us even more is our meditation on the parables of judgement. I thought I would offer them to you before the ones about *return* and *call*, because they are the ones we perhaps usually put aside. However, by way of introduction, I would like to emphasise the opportunity we are given during the retreat for a more extensive penitential conversation where the acts of the penitent are given greater depth.

The *penitential conversation* is where the time for confession is experienced very much in the context of the Church, beginning with thanksgiving and gratitude for God's gifts; this is the best way of acknowledging our smallness, the wrong we have done, all the good we have neglected to do. This is the *confessio laudis*, which is then followed by the *confessio vitae*: not only a detailed list of sins but a presentation of what weighs upon us, what is simply ballast in our lives, what clips our wings. More than formal sins, we are dealing with feelings of antipathy, narrow-mindedness, defensiveness, bad moods, edginess, exhaustion, all the things that hinder us from following God's ways and are cause for so many daily sins, at least of a venial kind.

From *confessio vitae* we more to *confessio fidei*: faith in Jesus Christ the Saviour, whose precious blood purifies us and whose gift of the Spirit renews us. In faith we open ourselves to forgiveness, mercy, the kerygma of new life in Christ, and hence to the capacity for loving all our brothers and sisters.

The seventeen parables

The parables we will be reflecting on, refer to the last judgement, the last things, even though the word 'judgement' can distance us from them (we have other things to do right now, we'll think about it…). But we will be meditating seriously on the present, where judgement is not at some future point but already impacts on our life.

We will pose some simple questions to ourselves, similar to the ones for the parables of the seed. How many and which ones are they? What are they saying? What do the people listening to them need? Why these parables? At the conclusion, a note on Christian vigilance.

There are at least some fifteen or so parables of judgement. I will limit myself to listing them and I believe some of us will find us saying: This is a parable? I've never heard of it!

- *Mark 13:33-37*: the parable of the door-keeper:

> Beware, keep alert; for you do not know when the time will come. It is like [the parable starts here] a man going on a journey, when he leaves home and puts his slaves in charge, each with his work, and commands the doorkeeper to be on the watch. Therefore, keep awake – for you do not know when the master of the house will come, in the evening, or at midnight, or at cockcrow, or at dawn, or else he may find you asleep when he comes suddenly. And what I say to you I say to all: Keep awake!

It is a parable of judgement and places the accent on vigilance.

- *Mark 5:25-26* (with a parallel in Luke 12:58-59): the parable of the mutual settling of accounts. The antithesis of this is in 5:21: 'You have heard that it was said to those of ancient times, "you shall not murder…" but I say to you…' And them comes the very expressive little parable:

> Come to terms quickly with your accuser while you are on the way to court with him, or your accuser may hand you over to the judge, and the judge to the guard, and you will be thrown into prison. Truly I tell you, you will never get out until you have paid the last penny.

These words of Jesus could be interpreted as a very straightforward exhortation: do not quarrel too much! But in the light of the other things he has said, it probably has significance of the parable kind. By not quarrelling so as not to end up in the hands of a judge, what is proposed is to love others from now on without waiting for the last judgement, where we will be judged severely for how we dealt with charity toward others.

- *Luke 12:39-40, Matthew 24:43-44:* the thief in the night:

> If the owner of the house had known at what hour the thief was coming…

- *Luke 12:42-46, Matthew 24:45-51:* the servant, the faithful manager and the wicked slave.

> [Blessed is] the faithful and prudent manager whom his master will put in charge of his slaves, to give them their allowance of food at the proper time.

Instead:

> ...if he begins to beat the other slaves, men and women... the master of that slave will come...

- *Luke 19:12-27, Matthew 25:14-30*: the parable of the talents. The master will ask for an account at the end.
- *Matthew 13:47-50*: the parable of the net:

> The kingdom of heaven is like a net that was thrown into the sea and caught fish of every kind; when it was full, they drew it ashore, sat down, and put the good into baskets but threw out the bad.

At the end of time the angels will come and separate the evil from the righteous.

- *Matthew 18:23-25*: the parable of the unforgiving servant. The one in debt who is not merciful to others will be punished.

We are not considering here the parable of the labourers contracted to work in the vineyard at the end of the day, since while it is about a final account, its fundamental meaning depends on the summons rather than the judgement.

- *Matthew 25:13*: the parable of the ten bridesmaids. When the bridegroom comes, five are ready, and five are not.
- *Matthew 25:32-46*: While this lies outside the parable genre as such, it is a scene strictly tied to the last

judgement: the sheep, goats, their separation and the reason for it.

- *Luke 12:16-21:* the parable of the rich fool who thought he was well provided for by the year's harvest, builds larger barns and rejoices. Fool! He will die that night.

- *Luke 12:35-38:* the vigilant servants. Very similar to Matthew's faithful manager, here it is told in another way: 'Blessed are those slaves whom the master finds alert.'

- *Luke 13:6-9:* the parable of the barren fig tree could refer to judgement as Luke presents it.

- *Luke 13:24-30:* the parable of the narrow door. If you are not ready, the owner will shut the door and you will knock in vain because he will respond that he does not know you.

- *Luke 16:1-8:* the parable of the dishonest manager who makes friends when he has to render account to his master.

- *Luke 16:19-31:* Dives and Lazarus. In the end there will be no reversal of the situation.

To these fifteen parables I would add a further two:

- *Matthew 22:1-10:* the wedding banquet. The first part is a parable of call, invitation. But in the last part, when the king comes in to see the guests and notes that one of them does not have a wedding garment, it becomes a parable of judgement.

- Bound up very much with language of the parable is the comparison with Noah and Lot in *Luke 17:26-37*. It is very interesting because it shows that Jesus does not stick to literary rules – only comparisons or only parables – but moves between both with great freedom. Let us read it:

> Just as it was in the days of Noah, so too it will be in the days of the Son of Man. They were eating and drinking, and marrying and being given in marriage, until the day Noah entered the ark and the flood came and destroyed all of them. Likewise just as it was in the days of Lot: they were eating and drinking, buying and selling, planting and building…

Paul's words in *1 Corinthians* 7:29-30 come to mind: 'Let even those who have wives be as though they had none… and those who buy as though they had no possessions… for the present form of this world is passing away.' This is the figure of speech used by Jesus as a warning.

> …but on the day that Lot left Sodom, it rained fire and sulphur from heaven and destroyed all of them – it will be like that on the day that the Son of Man is revealed.

Among all the material I have listed, you could choose one or other of the parables as your work of personal reflection.

Basic themes

I will quickly spell out four themes:

1. Judgement and its serious nature. There is a judgement on history that is inevitable and serious. This judgement is part of the kingdom of God and implies not only the kingdom of Yahweh (sins are forgiven, new life offered, unity with the Father is given out of love), but also that those who do not believe will perish, those who do not accept are lost, and those who do not attach themselves to this anchor of salvation will drown. The seriousness of the judgement corresponds to the seriousness of the offer, the totality of God's love revealed in Christ.

2. The theme of the return: the master goes away, comes back; the master arrives at the unexpected moment.

3. The theme of vigilance: not only a warning regarding the past – you must be vigilant because you know here, now, neither the day nor the hour, and any moment could be the moment of judgement.

4. The theme of the need for works: especially works of charity, generous love, talents, to bear fruit. The servant must treat the other servants well, not beat them, not abuse them. Come to agreement with the other before going to the judge (forgiveness and love); make friends with the mammon of iniquity (alms-giving); the servant who forgives the debt of 10,000 talents should have forgiven the 100 talents owed him by the other servant (mercy). The exhortation, then, becomes a strong one: generous love, alms-giving, love for the poor are ways of responding to the judgement.

These are four fundamental themes on which it is necessary to reflect, compare ourselves with, pray over.

Who are the parables told to?

Reading and re-reading the parables of judgement, we arrive at a somewhat discouraging conclusion regarding the people Jesus had before him when he is telling them these parables.

1. They are people who are rather distracted where the word of God is concerned, people very much caught up in daily affairs: eating, drinking, making money. They are swamped, not just immersed, their head just above water, swamped by worldly concerns and little concerned about the kingdom: who knows if it will come, if there will be a hereafter; the master continues to delay, and one would not even know if he was coming at all.

2. They are people who are very much concerned about themselves, even if not too worried about God. They lord it over others, are hard on their neighbours, know nothing of mercy. They take advantage of what they have to oppress their fellow human beings, do not help them. The unforgiving servant is typical of these kinds of people.

3. They believe they need render account to no one, like the rich fool – relax, eat, drink and be merry. They believe life is about what a man has, and not that it has meaning only for what is of value in God's eyes.

What does such an audience need? It needs shaking up in salutary fashion. It has to be reminded of the seriousness of God's demands and their finality: one cannot escape them. Either accept the kingdom or it will reject you; if it rejects you, you are lost, your life is under judgement because nothing can escape the seriousness of God's judgement on human history.

The people need to learn, then, that human beings are not worth something because of the goods they possess, and that more serious use of these goods is an opportunity to be charitable, merciful, to disseminate good around them. Today we speak of justice as an expression of charity. Perhaps we could add that these people need to understand that God is their supreme good, that the kingdom offers them the unique opportunity for bringing about genuine good, that outside this possibility human beings will not fulfil who they are but are heading for damnation.

Jesus points to this teaching when preaching with the parables of judgement, and we need to recognise that it is a rather harsh form of preaching. Perhaps this is why we easily put it aside, even for ourselves: we prefer encouragement to do good, to be better, to make some progress. Nevertheless, we need to be aware that Jesus told these parables and there was clearly a reason for it.

Why did Jesus tell them?

We are coming even closer to our original question as to why Jesus spoke in parables. Why these particular parables?

The reason here is probably is not the same as the one that emerged from the parables of the seed; there was suspicion and controversy to overcome.

In the parables of judgement, Jesus had to take account of spiritual and moral obstinacy. So he tried to shake the people out of this in all sorts of ways, beginning with ideas accessible to them: the servant waiting for his master; the home owner who fears the thief at night; the rich man who accumulates wealth and dies suddenly; the man being sued who does not come to terms with the one suing him and will end up losing all his money in court.

They are parables the people easily understand, and they help them appreciate the urgency and seriousness of God's judgement.

We can try to grasp what was going on in Jesus' heart while he was telling them.

1. First of all, *the clear primacy of God*. Jesus wants to insist that there is an absolute primacy of God over history, the human being, situations, goods. God must be recognised as God: 'Hallowed be thy name.'

2. The certainty that God is the supreme good offered to human beings: 'Thy kingdom come.' It is the supreme good that brings inevitable judgement, since it is not an optional good but an absolute one, and its opposite is *no good* for the human being. The offer of this good is so pressing (since it is from God who reveals himself) that it puts the one who rejects it in a state of damnation, in the deepest existential misery. Jesus feels the need to warn human beings with all the love possible: look at how grave, how serious your situation is; perhaps it is full of possibilities but is it risky; your freedom is an insistent, unavoidable responsibility and you cannot treat it almost as if it were a game.

Everyone has to apply Jesus' words to their actual life. My life, with its talents, is an absolutely serious invitation that God offers me of being in the kingdom, in fullness of communion with him and others; or it will become a rejection of this fullness. The rejection comes into play in my response to the call, and this is why we sometimes find the theme of the call in parables of judgement. The call is addressed to each person according to what they can give, and it is the concrete measure of the relationship with every other person.

Inner vigilance

The New Testament draws the practical conclusion of Christian vigilance from the parables of judgement. *To be vigilant means* staying alert under the emblem of God's supremacy, the fullness of his offer, the risk of betraying his trust. Christian vigilance is the situation of someone who is aware of this and lives it out in the everyday context.

We can explore the theme with some references, first of all, to the Greek Fathers and spiritual teachers from the East who speak of inner vigilance or custody of the heart. It is an understanding of New Testament vigilance at an inner, psychological level: 'Stay awake and pray so as not to fall into temptation: the spirit is willing but the flesh is weak'; words often repeated by Jesus in the final period of his life on earth.

Inner vigilance or custody of the heart means constant attention to thoughts, feelings, fantasies, judgements: the 'tangle' they become within us. Clearly we have no intention of indulging in psychoanalysis, probing the depths of consciousness. But, we can exercise some sort of surveillance over this 'inner world' of ours, applying the brake to the uproar of images that often whirl within us, and which are often the most common enemy of prayer, especially continuous prayer. The Fathers from the East link continuous prayer – the Jesus Prayer – with custody of the heart, closing the door of our inner senses in the belief that without inner vigilance, prayer of the heart cannot flourish. Vice versa, prayer of the heart is a means of vigilance, replacing the din of imagination and fears with begging for Jesus' mercy in the depths of our being. Jesus fills the heart, the imagination, the feelings of the one praying this way, becoming a reason for prayer. It is sometimes expressed in formulas but more often it is just being in God's sight, walking like Abraham in God's presence.

We often lament the fact that we do not know how to pray, and perhaps one of the reasons is actually the lack of vigilance of the heart; a vigilance that is very gentle, restful, and I would also say bracing, able to cure various kinds of nervous exhaustion. These mostly derive from a mixture of contrasting feelings we find impossible to block out. It is gentle, restful, and constructive in a person because it is neither the vigilance of the servant nor of the master.

The servant's vigilance is apprehensive: the master is about to come and we try to behave well, otherwise he will make us pay for it.

The master's vigilance really comes from fear: the thief will come so I need to put padlocks on the doors.

Jesus certainly recommends both kinds, but in the desire that they become the vigilance of the bride, of someone who knows the bridegroom is always there, always ready, already at the door. This vigilance strengthens the heart in affection because it has us live in anticipation – expectation of the one who is our life, our happiness, our fullness. In this sense, vigilance is a reason for deep inner peace, serenity, healing of the disordered movements of the heart, the spirit, the senses. We need to get on with the task of living this way, humbly asking the Lord for it in prayer as one of the fruits of the parables of judgement.

WHY JESUS SPOKE IN PARABLES

In this meditation, I would like to get to what I would say is almost the deepest understanding of parable. Why is parable possible? It is a difficult question, maybe even a pretentious one: I will try to offer some reflections that you can then personally explore further.

What parable is

Up till now, we have spoken of parables without having clearly defined them because it was better to start with an examination of what the gospel calls parables before trying to understand their nature. On the other hand, we have seen that Jesus was very free in telling them and did not follow any strict rules; it is really this fact that makes it more difficult to answer the question. It seems to me that the definition of parable includes at least four requirements:

1. *A story needs to be told, facts recounted one after the other; that is, an integrated or complete narrative.* The parable is not simply a static picture but needs a story on the move. We think, for example, of the coin that is lost then found: the woman loses it, looks for it, finds it again, rejoices. Sometimes, the narrative is very brief. Sometimes longer; what counts is that it includes moments that follow one another.

2. *'Veritas sublimior': it must contain a higher truth.* For example, if Jesus' words, 'Come to terms quickly with your accuser while you are on the way to court with him, or your accuser may hand you over to the judge,' were taken only as a moral principle (do not waste time and money!), there is no parable. But if I understand the story in the sense that, just as it is better to come to terms with your opponent in order not to pay much more later, then (and here is the higher truth) it is better not to come unprepared before God's judgement, but to prepare ourselves from now on through charity, almsgiving, mercy, forgiveness. Now we have a parable. By saying one thing, every parable should state something higher, make the leap from below to above, and this is its power.

3. *'A figurative approach'; a concrete symbolism is necessary.* Agricultural symbols, symbols of human work, how a father treats his son, fishing: figurative, sensible, tangible elements with colour, body, a real story of their own. The parable always starts out from things that can be said. By painting a picture of them or telling them in such a way they can be pictured, or by carrying them out in action, like a mime.

4. *'Per oppositionem vel compositionem veritatis et figurae,' the parable works on parallels, likeness, oppositions.* Between the earthly, visible reality and the higher truth there is a parallel, likeness or opposition.

The parable, then, is simple to tell, but it is difficult and complex in its meaning, and its richness comes from the fact that it expresses somewhat polished ideas. We would not tell parables to little children, for example. We would give them some examples, make some comparisons; the parable, on the other hand, requires a certain adult wisdom, reflection on life and what is greater than life, a comparison between one and the other. We could say that parables express something which is cultural and full of wisdom.

Why Jesus could speak in parables

Keeping in mind the four characteristics we have explained, we ask ourselves why it was appropriate for Jesus to use this language of parable, and why he can use it.

In my research, I have found some reasons that seem to throw light on this, even if they are not easy to put into words. First of all, they need to be considered as a whole, not each exclusively:

1. Jesus could speak in parables *because there is an analogy between body and spirit*. That is, it is possible to explain spiritual things (I am not talking about the supernatural), invisible things, through visible realities. It is possible to lead someone to knowledge of something beyond words through figurative language. We read in Preface I for The Nativity of the Lord: '... as we recognise in him God made visible, we may be caught up through him in love of things invisible.' There is a proportion between body and spirit, because the spiritual, mental, intellectual part of the human being is in strict correlation with, in a parallel of sorts, with the bodily part. It seems simple enough, but this claim has very extensive consequences for culture, literature, how we express ourselves. Without going to a parable, I will give you an immediate example: I cannot visually picture the intellectual development of an individual, but by thinking of a journey or climbing a mountain, I am able to say what intellectual, spiritual, cultural development is because it is proportionate to walking that requires one to take step after step.

2. Jesus could tell parables *because there is some degree of proportion between the world, history and the mystery of the kingdom.* Here we make an important leap, for example, that some of our Protestant brothers and sisters may struggle to make. Protestants – at least those of a more rigid Protestant belief – are led by a spirit that sees the reality of God as almost alienated from that of the world: God has his will, his mystery, his word and is so far above us that he cannot be compared to human realities. A certain kind of spiritualism or evangelism found in the Protestant world cannot admit of any proportion between human affairs and the kingdom of God.

In reality, the heart of biblical teaching, as well as the substance and life of the Catholic Church, is bound up with the certainty that there is proportion between the world, history, and the mystery of the kingdom. Thus, it is possible to reflect on the mystery of the seed, its growth, and compare this to growth of the Word of God. Being able to do so shows the unity of creation and the relationship between the plan of creation and the plan of redemption. The Prophet Ezekiel, for example, can compare a story about desert dwellers – the little foundling girl left bloodied in the desert, picked up and clothed and adorned with ornaments (Ezek 16) – with God's behaviour towards his people, because there is an affinity of sentiments, human ways of acting throughout history, and the mystery of God.

The parable teaches us, then, that we can know something of the mystery of God through human things. This is why we struggle to create parables (even though we should do so!): Jesus tells them as an inspired author who knows God, but for us it is a risk. Jesus knows the mystery of the kingdom and when he explains, 'The kingdom of God is like….' He is giving us an immense gift.

We would never dare do it. Our experience of God is so lacking, our faith so weak that we would end up projecting ourselves in our parables and our subjective ideas about God!

3. Jesus can tell parables *because God's deeds can be narrated.* It is a further step. It seems strange, but God has a history of his own. Natural religions do not admit it, maintaining that God is beyond everything, inaccessible, invisible, equal only to himself. Instead, the Christian revelation teaches that God is a story, a person, freedom, and in his own way can have a history. In fact, it speaks of the 'history of the Trinity.'

How can the Trinity, that has existed forever, have a history? Because it is put into words, communicated, revealed, and this is why God's deeds can be told through the recounting of human deeds. The parable of the prodigal son, starting from the tenderness of a father for his son who was lost then returns, torn and heart-stricken, tells us something about God: the fact that God welcomes us mercifully and freely. How could we know this if it were not possible to tell God's story?

4. Jesus can tell parables *because there are contrasts between the history of the world and the mystery of the kingdom.* They are not two equal realities. They can be compared but there is a contrast and it is this that the parable often plays upon. For example, the parable of the vineyard owner who takes on labourers at different times of the day and then gives everyone the same wage, lets us see that things are different in the eyes of God from the way they are with us. We can never quite fully justify the vineyard owner's behaviour. Jesus teaches us that the mystery of the Father is so great, so freely given, as not to make distinctions in the gift. Hence, we are worthless

servants. Through revealed comparisons, we are introduced to an understanding of some aspect of the mystery of the kingdom: when it speaks of a hundredfold in the parable of the seed, the reference is to the mystery of the kingdom, not to the story of the world, because the seed has an incredible output that the world does not know about. By looking at the world, we discover the mystery of God, but it has to be revealed to us.

5. Jesus can tell parables *because he is someone who meditates on the mystery*. He knows the mystery of God perfectly, because he is God, and he also knows the mystery of humankind perfectly, because he is a man. We find the mystery of the incarnate Word in his manner of speaking: by means of parable, Jesus takes humankind, grasps hold of it and brings it into the mystery of God, linking the two mysteries in the unity of his person.

We can pause here, because the connection between the mystery of the evangelical word and the Incarnation needs to be explored in prayer and contemplation.

The importance of lectio divina

At this point, it is easy to understand the importance of the *lectio divina* we are doing over these days. *Lectio divina* is an exercise in listening to the Word, grasping the mystery of the incarnate Word, and then penetrating the mystery of God himself. There is no deeply understood Christian life without *lectio divina*. Vatican II's Constitution *Dei Verbum* (Chapter 6) stated this clearly, and probably twenty years later, we have not fully accepted it. This is why it seems to me to be useful to speak about it in the hope that after the retreat, you will continue to practise *lectio divina*, a term difficult to translate, but drawn from the patristic tradition and meaning, literally, divine reading. It is reading the Scriptures in a spirit of prayer as God's Word, in a spirit of humble attention to this Word as it speaks to us in the context of our life, and within the framework of the Church and its teaching. So it is not a private reading, not study, not a cultural tool: it is a true and proper occasion of prayer; in some monastic traditions, along with the Office, it is the prayer *par excellence*.

Lectio divina is a complex, gradual activity, made up of stages or successive moments. I will try to explain these as completely as possible.

1. The first step is the *lectio*. This means reading and rereading the text so that its most significant structural elements emerge. We often say, for example, that the parable of the sower is one we already know, so it has little else to tell us. But, if we read it carefully – as we have done together – we discover so many insights that had escaped us. I always suggest to young people to read 'pen in hand', underlining verbs, active tenses, nouns, adjectives, etc. Little by little, the text acquires deeper meaning. Sometimes, our meditation on the Scriptures is dry, because we read them hurriedly, without pause, or because our greatest concern is to immediately think of comments, explanations, without making the personal effort to read carefully.

After analysing the passage and its elements, we can look for other pages that record similar situations in the Old or New Testaments. The *lectio* is broadened, events or biblical figures (David, Moses, Abraham) come to mind, the text we are reading is clarified by an attitude of Jesus on one occasion or by a word of St Paul on another.

The work of *lectio* is not exegesis properly so called, because exegesis has precise technical rules coming from original texts: it studies the oral and written prehistory of the passage. *Lectio* instead seeks to come into contact with the text itself.

2. The *Meditatio* is the next step, and presumes that the text has been read, reread and internalised. To meditate means to ruminate, reflect on the biblical page by means of some questions or, in other words, by considering its permanent values. From what Jesus said two thousand years ago, or what Abraham did three thousand years ago, I need to seize upon some perennial values. What are they? Why are they important? What do they mean today? What is their significance for me? And so, we enter into a dialogue with the Word of God, asking: 'What is it telling me? What attitude, Lord, are you suggesting to me through this text? What attitude should I be on my guard against? What mystery about yourself, Lord, are you revealing to me? What depths of the human heart are being discovered?'

3. The *oratio* is the third moment. At a certain point of the *meditatio* I am ready to pray. Really though, I can pray from the outset: I pray to get to know Jesus who is speaking to me in this passage. I can pray to understand its values. Nevertheless, and most importantly, prayer *begins* at a certain moment. 'Lord, I do not know you. I do not have this virtue. I cannot understand this behaviour of yours, it is too much for me.'

4. The prayer that starts out from the text tends to become *contemplatio*, or contemplation. Ignoring the details, we contemplate the mystery of God at the heart of every page of the Bible, the mystery of the Trinity, the Father, Son, Holy Spirit. We contemplate it in a simple conversation that is adoration, praise, offering, thanksgiving, a request for grace or even a humble glance; not the impoverished glance of someone who looks and no longer knows what to do, but a glance enriched by the whole Word we are meditating upon, a glance that is a response to the Word.

If *lectio* is active listening, *contemplatio* is a passive moment of intimacy. It is important because in fact, only at the level of this intimacy do we begin to know God in experience, in our heart, and not only through our intellect. The Lord can certainly call us to contemplation without passing through the words of Scripture, but ordinarily it is the Scriptures that arouse faith in the Word in us and, from faith, contemplation.

These four steps could be enough, but to be more complete we should point out some of the benefits of contemplation.

5. The most immediate benefit is *consolatio*. This is a New Testament term (consolation or *paraclesis*) and means a deep inner joy, the taste for things of God, the taste for God as God, the taste for truth, chastity, sacrifice, love. It is a taste of the fruits of the Holy Spirit, a kind of instinctive shared nature with the gospel values that *lectio* has helped us discover, *meditatio* has confronted us with, *contemplatio* has suggested to us in the person of Jesus and now, at this moment of consolation, they are integrated within our being. Because of this *consolatio*, the saints achieved so many good works, endured countless apostolic labours, and the martyrs faced persecution.

6. *Consolatio* is followed by the specific attitude of the New Testament called *discretio*, discernment. Much has been said about this in Italy at the Loreto Church Conference when they spoke of spiritual and pastoral discernment. To understand it, however, it is necessary to bring it into relationship with *lectio divina*.

Discernment is the inner capacity to perceive where the Spirit of God is at work, the Spirit of the Gospel, the Spirit of Christ: in situations, decisions, events, problems. And it is also perceiving where the spirit of Satan, his lies, trickery, bitterness, confusion, is at work. When it is given to us through an almost instinctive and ongoing spiritual sensitivity, discernment is called the gift of discernment of spirits. St Paul prays that it be given to his followers, and it is essential for whomever has responsibilities.

Those who have few choices to make (a child, a young boy or girl, anyone with a rather confined existence) already have their choices, and if they live in obedience to them, they are sanctified through them. Whoever has to make pastoral, apostolic choices has very great need of this discernment to understand where the Spirit of Christ is at work and where the spirit of Satan is deceiving us: here is something right, here is evangelical sacrifice, here is holiness, here is sincere obedience, while here, instead, is falsity, cunning, mere appearance, rhetoric; here is boastfulness, things that seem okay but really are bad.

Discernment never finishes, because we constantly find situations, problems, difficulties along our personal journey that cannot be mechanically solved with a computer but need to be tackled each time with the Spirit of Jesus. Sometimes, especially in extreme cases, there are very complicated moral situations that give rise to endless discussions among moralists. But the pastor is forced to make choices leaving the moralists to keep on discussing, and perhaps can only make them by using spiritual discernment.

7. *Deliberatio* is the next step after *discretio*, and indicates a concrete, gospel-based choice. Every great Christian choice, in particular the choices Religious make, like poverty, obedience, chastity, come from our spiritual conformity with Christ. We often look for the reasons behind the evangelical counsels, forgetting that the fundamental one is this conformity with Christ, that is conformity with the Father. It is true that there are other plausible motives and convincing ones, but they are not sufficient to act upon if there is not the spiritual stimulus to encourage and work on us. This is why a religious vocation is always the work of the Holy Spirit, and those in search of vocations today know it: they toss out a net here and there and then see that their hopes are not fulfilled. It is only the inner power of the Spirit that leads one to choose the evangelical life; otherwise it is not a true evangelical choice.

8. The final step is *actio*, the evangelical action following on from the choice from *deliberatio*.

These eight moments or occasions could be summed up in other words: the time of *ascent (lectio, meditatio, oratio)*, the *peak (contemplatio)*, the *descent (consolatio, discretio, deliberatio, actio)*. This is the resolution of the famous prayer-action dilemma. They are not two parallel or opposite things at all, because evangelical action comes from the evangelical prayer of the Scriptures. They are two moments of a single movement, conforming oneself to the movement of Christ toward our humanity, and to Christ's choices and actions.

Lectio divina thus constitutes the warp and woof of the whole spiritual life of the Church, the root of Christian spirituality, and is not exclusive of any kind of spirituality. A Christian spirituality not based on the Scriptures can only survive with difficulty in a complex world like ours. It is a difficult, disintegrated and disoriented world. Without the exercise of *lectio divina,* the Christian will always have a childish faith that is pulled apart by life. This is why I wanted to pause and explain it in such a way that you can be of help to others.

A question arises: where and how to do *lectio divina?* Can any Scripture help us? But the Bible has an order, a structure to it. It is not a collection of books stuck together by accident. It is certainly the Church, through the liturgical year with Easter at the centre, that gives us the order, structure, values of Scripture. Therefore, with the new lectionary it is very advisable to practise *lectio divina* by following the liturgical readings of the day. Reading the Scriptures in the Church, in accordance with the teaching of the Popes, the Magisterium, is equivalent to ordering what are sometimes just our own rough ideas. Reading the Scriptures in the Church's liturgical life means allowing ourselves to be formed on a journey of the catechumenate with the emphases that the liturgy proposes to the Christian year after year through its symbols.

A simple example of lectio divina

We are still in the time dedicated to confession. I would like to read you an example of *lectio divina* that entered one individual's heart. I am talking about some lines from a man facing many years of prison, so he is writing in the context of unprecedented suffering of an obscure life he sees ahead. This prisoner, a former terrorist, had read the little book of meditations on Psalm 50 (51) from talks I gave last year to young people for the School of Prayer. He paraphrased the *Miserere* by going back over his own journey and experiencing the sentiments of the penitent very profoundly.

> 'Give me your grace, O God, according to your steadfast love. Blot out my rebellion against your order, in great love from the depths of your being, and your ability to immerse yourself in my situation. Wash me from my iniquity; pull me out of my confusion to an alternative project. Today, you rejoice over me, you accept me as I am. You reveal yourself to me so that I can come to know you. Help me to accept others as you accept me. [This is almost heroic in prison, because it is very difficult to accept oneself in a place often based on mutual violence.] Grant me strength and suggest what I can do for their good and to change them for the better. You know me, you look at me to question me; you query me and I listen to your reproach. [You see how he bears in mind the way the psalm develops]. I know my transgressions; my sin is ever before me. I have sinned in what I have done to others and to nature. Against you, against you alone, I have sinned! In examining my responsibilities, I do not lose heart uselessly but I converse with you. How was it possible to do what is evil in your eyes, to your love? Yet I did so! I ask myself daily what weighs on me

and makes me uneasy, how I should have behaved differently. If you were only a judge, there would be no escape for me; but you are the wounded party and your judgement is forgiveness. My sorrow comes from this lack of proportion: how could I offend the one who still exchanges friendship with me? And how many times I offend you by ignoring a relationship with others! I too, when I consider I have been hurt, would like to repay that with forgiveness and friendship.

Indeed, I was born guilty, my mother conceived me in the sin of the world, but you love the truth also in my dark heart and in its intimacy, you teach me hope, your order, your warmth, your plan of salvation. Help me discover, and urge me on towards the truth of who I am. Purify me and I shall be clean, wash me and I shall be whiter than snow. Hide your face from my sins and blot out all my iniquities. Create in me a clean heart, put a steadfast spirit in me, do not cast me away from your presence and do not take your Holy Spirit from me. May I feel the joy of being loved, accepted again, saved: in prayer, adoration, silence, and in music, dialogue about your Word; in contemplation, sacrifice, gift, renunciation, in my inner voice.

May the gift of your joy explode within me. Assured of your love and forgiveness, I ask you to strengthen me in ways different from what I have been. And as you have done for me, so do I know you can always correct and convert others.

Make me an instrument of salvation through forgiveness, friendship, testimony to joy. Give me the willingness and ability to admonish lovingly for the other's good. Give me confidence in your power to create new hearts. Help me to share in the generosity of your heart. I would like to be a witness to your mercy, to teach your ways and have sinners return to you.

I would like to proclaim your truth of salvation, embody it in daily practice, forgiving in turn, accompanying others, correcting them with love and humility.

I implore your mercy before all evil and every threat; I implore your counsel and the strength to give myself to resist evil. Free me from the offence I have caused, God my salvation.

I will praise your justice and declare your praise. The sacrifice acceptable to you is a contrite spirit, a broken and contrite heart you will not despise.

May the conversion of my heart be for me a commitment to social reconciliation. Help me to joyfully practise works of penance, useful not only to me but to humanity, for whose journey of conversion I share responsibility.'

THE PARABLES OF THE LOST AND FOUND

'Lord, grant us the grace
of avoiding the pitfall of self-neglect,
the pitfall of tiredness.
May we contemplate your face
and may this refresh us on our journey.
Help us also to avoid
being beached in the shallows of meditation.
See that beyond the things on which
we meditate we arrive at contemplation of you.
Revive and nurture our faith, our spirit.
Grant that we may be nimble, agile, serene of heart,
so that in the quiet and silence of your being
we can hear the wonders of your word.'

We would like to try to hear the wonders of God's Word in the parables of the lost and found. If we bear in mind especially the story of the prodigal son, we can also call them parables of return, but in the others the theme of loss and rediscovery is stressed more. Moreover, the story of the prodigal son ends with the father's exclamation: 'this brother of yours was dead and has come to life, he was lost and has been found' (Lk 15:32).

Parables told and parables lived

Which and how many are these parables?
- *Luke* 15:4-7: the lost and found sheep;
- *Luke* 15:8-10: the lost and found coin;
- *Luke* 15:11-32: the lost and found son.

These three are the best known, and only the one about the lost and found sheep has a parallel in Matthew 18:12-14.

- *Luke* 18:9-14 – the story of the Pharisee and the publican. It is from the same kind of discourse as Luke's other three.

At first glance we could stop here, noting how few of them there are by comparison, for example, with the seventeen parables of judgement or vigilance. We could ask ourselves if Mark really did not have any lost and found parables. But we should recall the most mysterious part of the parable of the murderous tenants (Mk 12:1-8).

- *Mark* 12:6: it tells us about the owner who had sent along various servants, some who were ill-treated, others killed: 'He still had one other, a beloved son. Finally, he sent him to them, saying, 'They will respect my son.' It seems to me that this verse has a very special flavour and highlights the sense of seeking out what has been lost: the tenants are lost and the owner does everything to recover them to the point of risking his own son's life. Although in itself it is a parable of judgement, the theme of lost and found needs to be emphasised.

- I would then add the parable of the Great Dinner that belongs to the double tradition, but Luke, especially, develops it according to the aspect that interests us:

> So, the slaves returned and reported this to his master. Then the owner of the house became angry

and said to his slave, 'Go out at once into the streets and lanes of the town and bring in the poor, the crippled, the blind and the lame.' And the slave said, 'Sir, what you ordered has been done and there is still room.' Then the master said to the slave, 'Go out into the roads and lanes, and compel people to come in, so that my house may be filled' (Lk 14:21-23).

The basic theme is one of call, invitation. Nevertheless, the insistence of those whom nobody would invite to a dinner, even the invitation to people who live outside the city along the hedgerows – therefore people of ill-repute – is within the bounds of the parables of the lost and found, as we will see more clearly.

It also seems the right moment to extend our discussion, leaving aside the strictly literal meaning of parables of the kingdom, to keep in mind what in Hebrew is the word *'mashál'* or a wise saying, figurative language: stories told or lived, parables in action. These are *mashál*, so long as they have a tendency toward the higher meaning that we have seen to be a feature of the parable. This enables us to continue with our list:

- *Mark 2:15-17*: the symbolic gesture of Jesus eating with sinners:

> And as he sat at dinner in Levi's house, many tax collectors and sinners were also sitting with Jesus and his disciples – for there were many who followed him. When the scribes of the Pharisees saw that he was eating with sinners and

tax collectors, they said to his disciples, 'Why does he eat with tax collectors and sinners?' When Jesus heard this, he said to them, 'Those of you who are well have no need of a physician, but those who are sick: I have come to call not the righteous but sinners.'

That it may be a kind of parable, is also indicated by the question it gives rise to for the Pharisees. Jesus' gesture goes well beyond mere gesture. It is a parable in action that belongs to the theme of the lost and found.

- *Mark 2:14*: the call of Levi, the publican seated at his tax booth, thus despised by the general populace, is a parable of seeking what is lost.

- *John 4*: Jesus' conversation with the Samaritan woman leaves the disciples dumbfounded. It is a sign of his seeking out someone who is distant, someone generally considered to be of no 'interest' (because she is a Samaritan and a woman).

- Along similar lines, *Mark 2:1-12*: the healing of the paralytic, a sign of the remission of sins. Although it is an act of mercy, it stresses Jesus' interest in what is lost. The theme of the lost and found is strongly part of Jesus' symbolic way of acting, parable in action, and not only in his preaching.

- *Mark 3:1-6*: the healing of a man with a withered hand, on a Sabbath day, is a sign of how Jesus takes an interest in human beings in their poverty. He poses a question at the heart of this scene: 'Is it lawful to do good or to do harm on the Sabbath, to save life or to kill? But they were silent.' Jesus' attention to this lost, suffering human being goes beyond social taboos and their restrictiveness or religious connotations.

- *Mark 1:41:* 'Moved with pity, Jesus stretched out his hand and touched him.' Touching a leper, a gesture not permissible in itself, makes him unclean. It is another parable of concern for what is lost.

- *Luke 13:15:* The crippled woman, cured on a Sabbath day. Jesus explains that his action has a meaning that goes beyond a simple act of benevolence:

> You hypocrites! Does not each of you on a Sabbath day untie his ox or donkey from the manger and lead it away to give it water? And ought not this woman, a daughter of Abraham, whom Satan bound for eighteen long years, be set free from this bondage on the sabbath day?

- *Mark 2:19:* Jesus explains why his disciples do not fast, as a parable of something deeper: 'Jesus said to them, "The wedding guests cannot fast while the bridegroom is with them, can they?" It is a symbolic act pointing to the fact that certain rules are superseded by Jesus' presence.

I leave it up to you to continue the search for stories in action that express the theme of the lost and found. We can now ask ourselves about their content, what are they saying.

I would emphasise four basic things.

1. *Something has been lost* (a person, a thing, an animal). When it is a person, the concept is extended: sinners, the marginalised, outcasts, individuals shown little respect, without social influence – the poor, the lame, the crippled who are invited to the dinner and who cannot return the invitation. From people, we move to situations: caste taboos,

social and cultural barriers, which legitimise the rejection of some, compared to others.

2. *What is lost is carefully sought out...*

3. *Lovingly accepted...*

4. *And finally, happily refound.* The theme of joy at this rediscovery is very much stressed, especially in Luke 15: 'I tell you, there will be more joy in heaven over one sinner who repents then over ninety-nine righteous persons who need no repentance' (v. 7). 'I tell you, there is joy in the presence of the angels of God over one sinner who repents' (v. 10). 'Quickly, bring out a robe – the best one – and put it on him; put a ring on his finger and sandals on his feet. And get the fatted calf and kill it and let us eat and celebrate.' And they begin to celebrate. The other one heard the music, the dancing… (v. 22). Joy, a banquet, feasting, music, dance are tied to the rediscovery of the lost one.

An audience with a jaundiced eye

Who are the recipients of this teaching in parables whether narrated or shown in action? The gospel gives us some precise indications.

1. Jesus has an *audience of envious grumblers* before him. These grumblers are pointed out in Luke 15:1-2:

> Now all the tax collectors and sinners were coming near to listen to him. And the Pharisees and the scribes were grumbling and saying, 'This fellow welcomes sinners and eats with them.' Then he told them this parable.

We see the envious types in Matthew 9:10-11:

> And as he sat at dinner in the house, many tax collectors and sinners came and were sitting with him and his disciples. When the Pharisees saw this, they said to his disciples, 'Why does your teacher eat with tax collectors and sinners?'

This is just envious grumbling: why not with us? Why with him?

2. *The envious grumblers are insiders*, not outsiders. The Pharisees are fully at home in the Jewish religion. We find this domestic jealousy expressed in parable and, dramatically, in the second part of the story of the prodigal son where the older son rebels:

> [The servant] replied, 'Your brother has come, and your father has killed the fatted calf, because he has got him back safe and sound.' Then he became angry and refused to go in (Lk 15:27-28).

3. *The insiders who believe they know the Father*. The older brother believes he knows his father and is wondering what he is doing. 'Listen! For all these years I have been working like a slave for you, and I have never disobeyed your command; yet, you have never given me even a young goat so that I might celebrate with my friends' (v. 29). The people who believe they know God say: how come he behaves like this? He is unjust and should absolutely not do this. He never did so with me and I know him and have served him for many years.'

4. *A respectable people.* Luke premises the parable of the Pharisee and the publican with a comment: 'He also told this parable to some who trusted in themselves that they were righteous and regarded others with contempt' (18:9).

This is the complete picture given to us by the gospel of the people Jesus is addressing. We could characterise this audience by saying it is a people with a jaundiced eye. We take the image from the parable of the labourers sent to work in the vineyard over various hours of the day (*Mt* 20) where the landlord concludes his speech to his 'friend' who complains he has worked all day and received the same wage as the others: 'Or are you envious because I am generous?' (*v.* 15). In the Greek text, this word 'envious' is '*ofthalmòs sou ponerós,*' your eye is evil, jaundiced. With the metaphor of the jaundiced eye, then, we can point to the kind of public Jesus is addressing.

A disconcerting revelation of God

What new idea about God is revealed by the parables of the lost and found? Undoubtedly, of all the parables, they are the most disconcerting. They communicate an idea of God which we do not know in human terms; and not only do we not know, but it creates a problem each time and we react immediately. But we can get to know the God of Jesus Christ especially through these parables, and other parables in action. I will try to express this new idea of God we are given, through a basic statement spelt out in five comments.

The statements: *God is interested in what is lost.* It seems easy to say but it is disconcerting when we really think about it, and it is full of consequences for our human existence.

1. *God seeks what is lost:* 'Which one of you, having a hundred sheep and losing one of them, does not leave the ninety-nine in the wilderness and *go after the one that is lost until he finds it?'* (Lk 15:4). 'Or what woman having ten silver coins, if she loses one of them, does not light a lamp, sweep the house and search carefully *until she finds it?'* (Lk 15:8). The woman's actions speak of the anguish of the search and the means employed in the search are expressed to indicate who God is. So, we have before us a revelation of Jesus Christ about God.

Matthew 12:11-21 can also be read in this context. Some verses of the passage are very controversial in the Church today, and in pastoral activity at the practical, rather than the theological level. Matthew makes a Christological summary of Jesus, Servant of Yahweh (quoting Isaiah 42:1-4) and of Jesus' interest in the sick. But reading Isaiah, we see that the sick are a symbol of what has been lost, of what has no social influence, of what is spontaneously marginalised, worth nothing. The sentence under discussion says: 'He will not wrangle or cry aloud nor will anyone hear his voice in the streets. He will not break a bruised reed or quench a smouldering wick *until he brings justice to victory*' (vv. 19-20). The expression 'until he/she has found it' in the parables of the sheep and the coin, led me to understand this passage from Matthew.

Every time we do not know how to act properly when faced with real cases (for example, to give or refuse the sacraments), the words of the Prophet quoted by Matthew bring out our uncertainty: 'He will not quench a smouldering wick.' Must we be harsh, intransigent, severe in sending away people who ask to be married in the Church without demonstrating serious intent, or would Jesus want more tolerance, more patience? After all, Jesus did not shout, did not raise his voice, so perhaps it is better not to quench the smouldering wick!

These rather facile and simplistic applications are understood better and in more evangelical detail, it seems to me, if we refer to the image of God seeking out those who are lost. God so much wants justice to triumph in us that he uses every means, including merciful, persevering, patient, careful, respectful searching. Not quenching the smouldering wick is not about taming religion. It is Jesus who, with infinite love, moves toward all the difficulties of the human being to overcome them with his focusing power. The passage in Matthew 20 indicates that God is interested in what is lost and seeks it out anxiously, flexibly, and with the capacity we find in the parables and the ways Jesus' actions are summed up.

2. God experiences joy at finding what was lost. If the gospel had not said it, we would not have dared say it. Jesus assures us that God experiences almost exorbitant joy, greater than what he feels for ninety-nine righteous individuals. Here, the father's words are perhaps the most beautiful of all: 'But we had to celebrate and rejoice, because this brother of yours was dead and has come to life; he was lost and has been found' (Lk 15:32). We know very little about God, but we know he experiences joy in finding someone lost.

3. God confronts his critics while standing by the lost. The father lovingly confronts the elder brother who is angry. He does so patiently, but he does confront him and begs no pardon for it, since it has to be done. Jesus confronts his critics to the point where they slander him: 'Look, a glutton and drunkard, a friend of tax collectors and sinners' (Mt 11:19).

He confronts the harshest criticism regarding his private life, his way of behaving. These criticisms come from jealousy. It is God himself who confronts them in Jesus. These criticisms are constantly and almost infallibly repeated. When attention began to be given to former terrorists, now prisoners, in Italy, there were immediately criticisms: what is this new way of thinking? These people are murderers who have made orphans of children and widows of wives. We need to leave them where they are to serve out their sentence! How come the Church is now interested in them, instead of thinking of the victims' families? Where will we end up? The Church is now thinking more about the undeserving types, than of the faithful who go to Church! The people criticising are also of the conforming kind. The truth is, that every time we present the image of God who seeks out the lost, people feel ill at ease.

4. *God risks his own Son for the Lost.* This is the mysterious emphasis of the parable of the murderous vineyard tenants that we have already read (*Mk* 12:6). We can't explore it here and I leave it to your work of personal reflection. God risks his own Son for people who don't deserve it.

5. *God is also interested in the single lost individual,* not just the lost in general. He is interested in one all alone. There is a degree of hyperbole in the first two parables in Luke 15. Jesus the shepherd leaves the ninety-nine sheep in the wilderness and goes in search of the one who is lost. This does not normally happen because the shepherd prefers to think of the safety of the ninety-nine and let the lost one go. It is very difficult for us to accept that he goes around until he finds the lost sheep, risking the other ninety-nine getting into strife or being stolen.

In the second parable, we see the woman make so much effort and celebrate with her neighbours and friends for finding just one coin out of the ten. This is implausible; we would understand it if she had lost nine, but her way of behaving seems excessive for only one.

The two parables are something of a paradox, so they can point to the mystery of God who is also interested in just one lost, insignificant soul without value, from whom nothing good can be expected. Clearly, it is not the intention that the many should be ignored, but it is a hyperbolic image of the incomprehensibility of the mystery of God.

I recall a conversation with a young political detainee who was clearly and simply telling me how he was going at a time of change, of recognition of his error, even though not yet at the point of a religious conversion. He explained that along with other terrorists he had spent years in a foolish dream, only seeing an ideology, ignoring the fact that there were individuals, and that he was risking his life for an ideology and leading a very dangerous life. At a certain point, seeing the attention Christian volunteers were giving to individuals, the affection they bore for him as an individual, he discovered the existence and value of the individual as such.

Awareness of the value of a person is the reflection of a divine attitude: God is also interested in the single, lost individual. For him, just one is like ninety-nine, is like everyone. From this truth flows the dignity of the human person that civil society is not accustomed to. Perhaps it proclaims it in words, but commonly speaking, in the most advanced of civil societies, the focus is on the whole, the totality, the group, and it does what it can for the individual.

There is a revelation of the living God in Christ's parables and actions, and also a revelation of the image of God impressed on the human being, of the dignity of every person, that can be realised without any revelation.

This is why the Christian ethic reaches very demanding heights, and is one that people do not understand, because they do not reach a precise idea of the absolute dignity of the human being at every stage or in every circumstance of their life: conception, birth, death; sickness, final agony, feeble-mindedness, dementia. It is very difficult in practice to reach this actual understanding.

In-house envy

From our meditations, we can draw a practical reflection on *envy in the Church*, a practical reflection resulting from the attitude of the elder brother in the parable of the prodigal. It is a kind of in-house envy and can be described as a jaundiced eye. The jaundiced eye – we have seen it in the parable of the labourers called to work at different times in the vineyard – also appears in the list of basic vices that come from a person's heart: 'Adultery, avarice, wickedness, deceit, licentiousness, envy [*ofthalmòs poneròs*], slander, pride, folly. All these evil things come from within, and they defile a person' (Mk 7:22-23). Coming from within, they are inevitably in all of us, even in members who make up the Church, not in the Church as the body of Christ.

1. *Envy, then, within the community,* in individuals, comparing one with another; envy between different groups, movements, parishes, movements *and* parishes. It is a huge field, one that offers opportunities for a jaundiced view of things. A better description could be to speak of *resentment and discomfort regarding the goodness of others,* including their

spiritual and apostolic goodness: we not only feel indignant because others have better cars, more houses, this or that, but because of their *spiritual, cultural, apostolic successes* that are not mine. This generates resentment that comes from evil desires, from the depths of the psyche.

The result of this discomfort is a further parallel and secondary attitude: *we are happy when things go wrong for others*. It was okay if they deserved it, but not everything that glitters is gold – you can see they were too proud! Listening to these sentiments, we immediately see that they are small-minded, vile, and we are sure they will never be in our heart. But in reality, if we examine our attitudes carefully – judgements, little barbed comments, certain ways of sidelining people – we see that resentment, discomfort at another's good, being happy when things go wrong for someone, are also at work in us at the level of judgements or choices. This happens because, deep down, there is a certain healthy root which is imitation, the will to do better and more: I am capable, I could do it, we could do it really well! The root is good but is sometimes spoiled, poisoned, or at least, eaten away at by resentment or despondency.

So, it is important to listen, listen to the gospel's warning: there is envy in us too because we are at home in the Church, religious people who feel we are in our place, we do good. It is much more subtle when people are upright and spiritual: there is nothing more subtle than spiritual pride, spiritual envy, nothing more devastating than so-called 'clerical hatred'. The sensitivity of the spirit is strictly tied to spiritual pride – one of the worst vices – to a taste for spiritual domination of others. This is a terrible threat to the life of the spirit. Even if all this only touches us lightly, not seriously, it is a kind of poisonous gas that makes the air unbreathable.

Sometimes I am amazed, moving around the Church, at how the jaundiced eye often prevents us from seeing the good that is there. I go somewhere, see really significant activities from a gospel point of view, and when I ask others about them, I hear that basically 'it is not much, we could do much better if...'; 'it would be significant but...' There is no appreciation, because there are suspicions, and this is why, at times, we have a diminished notion of the power of the Spirit in the Church: our eyes are fixed on our activities, our things, what we are doing, our method, our initiatives.

No surprise, then, that the Acts of the Apostles praises Barnabus very much. When he arrived in Antioch, *since he was good*, he saw God's grace and rejoiced. Vice versa, we know from Church history that entire missions collapsed because of various kinds of internal struggles (I am thinking of the China missions at the time of Matteo Ricci); jealousies, difficulties, problems which were then clothed in theology, created opposition such that it practically destroyed the apostolic work.

2. *What remedy for envy in the Church does the gospel point to?* Mark suggests it in the chapter of parables, in a passage we have not as yet read because it is always a bit of a mystery:

> And he said to them, 'Pay attention to what you hear; the measure you give will be the measure you get, and still more will be given you. For to those who have, more will be given; and from those who have nothing, even what they have will be taken away' (4:25-26).

The first sentence, as generic as it is, can be applied to so many situations, while the second, being rather vague, takes on a precise meaning in our context. The more we get involved, allow ourselves to be personally involved in the parables, the more we can receive, and the more we receive the more we will have. For what concerns us I would translate this as: the more we are aware of the immense gifts God has given us, the more we are ready to recognise them in others. If we do not learn to praise and recognise that so many deeds in our life, our circumstances, are not our merit, our efforts, our traditions, but are God's unlimited gifts, the more we will be led to recognise this elsewhere, because they are gifts of the very same Lord. But the more we personally appropriate something almost as if it were ours, it must not be let go of, it is our personal property, the result of our efforts – well then, the more we are led to envy others who perhaps with less effort seem to have more.

The Lord, then, suggests the contemplation of God's infinite mercy and tenderness as a remedy for jealousy. He fills us with good things to the point where we have no need to be envious of anyone. God could, if he wanted to, make us wiser than St Thomas, more penitent than St Aloysius Gonzaga, more zealous than St Francis Xavier. He has all these gifts for us and we can thank him for the ones he has given us, and will give us, and we can praise him in the gifts of our brothers and sisters.

JESUS' LIFE AS A PARABLE

'Holy Spirit, grant that we may understand
the mystery of Jesus' life.
Give us an understanding of his person,
that sublime understanding
for which Paul let everything else go
to know Jesus,
experience communion in his suffering,
share in his glory.
We ask you this
through the intercession of Mary, Mother of Jesus,
who knows Jesus with the perfection
and completeness of a mother
and with the perfection and completeness of
She who is full of grace.'

Mashál and parabolé

We have clarified what is meant by parable in the strict sense as a linguistic device, and have sought to extend the discussion, bearing in mind what *mashál* in Hebrew means. As well, the Greek word *parabolé* can help us in our work. Besides meaning 'parable', it implies other things: for example, it means juxtaposition, putting two things, two situations, two facts one beside the other; or the convergence of two stars in the Heavens; or even a meeting in a general sense. *Parabolé* is used, then, every time two things are brought together in some way.

Moreover, the Scriptures understand these meanings. The very real parable that Nathan tells David (2 Sam 12) is in fact called a *mashál*, a *parabolé*, as is the allegory of the eagle in Ezekiel 17. Here we see a much more elaborate development of the simple parable:

> The word of the LORD came to me: O mortal, propound a riddle, and speak an allegory to the house of Israel. Say: Thus, says the LORD GOD: a great eagle with great wings and long pinions, rich in plumage of many colours, came to the Lebanon. He took the top of the cedar… (Ezek 17:1-3).

This is a series of continuous metaphors also called parables. We have classified as parable certain symbolic actions, ways of acting of Jesus that indicate the mystery of God in search of what is lost.

We can read a clear example of symbolic action in the Old Testament, for example in Jeremiah 19:

> Thus, says the LORD: Go and buy a potter's earthenware jug. Take with you some of the elders of the people and some of the senior priests and go out to the valley of the son of Hinnom at the entry of the Potsherd Gate and proclaim there the words that I tell you … Then you shall break the jug in the sight of those who go with you, and shall say to them: Thus, says the LORD of hosts; so will I break this people and this city, as one breaks a potter's vessel, so that it can never be mended.

These symbolic actions can take the same name of parable in the Bible. We see it in two passages from the Letter to the Hebrews:

- *Hebrews 9:9:* The fact that the high priest comes in once a year, taking the blood he offers for himself and for the sins of the people 'is a symbol – *etis parabolé* – of the present time.' It is a way of showing something that is also valid today.
- *Hebrews 11:17-19:* 'By faith Abraham, when put to the test, offered up Isaac. He who had received the promises was ready to offer up his only son of whom he had been told, "It is through Isaac that descendants shall be named for you." He considered the fact that God is able even to raise someone from the dead – and figuratively speaking – *parabolé* – he did receive him back.' The note in the Jerusalem Bible explains that Israel's salvation is a symbol and parable of the general resurrection and also of the passion and resurrection of Christ.

The Scriptures invite us to broaden the concept of parable, so we would like to try to reflect on Jesus' life as a parable.

Jesus, parable of God's tender love

To understand Jesus' entire life as a parable, I am making some claims.

First of all, we will consider a typical parable in action, acknowledged by all the exegetes and usually considered within the framework of the parables; *the cursing of the withered fig tree* in Mark 11:12-14, 20-21:

> On the following day, when they came from Bethany, he was hungry. Seeing in the distance a fig tree in leaf, he went to see whether perhaps he

would find anything on it. When he came to it, he found nothing but leaves, for it was not the season for figs.

It is so clear that it is a symbolic act, that Mark hastens to add that it was not the season for figs. But Jesus' curse could not be about the poor plant!

> He said to it, 'May no one ever eat fruit from you again!' and his disciples heard it... In the morning as they passed by, they saw the fig tree withered away to its roots. Then Peter remembered and said to him, 'Rabbi, look! The fig tree that you cursed has withered!'

In its parallel version, in Matthew 21:19, the Jerusalem Bible explains: Jesus wanted to make a symbolic gesture in which the fig tree represents Israel, sterile and punished. Jesus, like Jeremiah, carried out symbolic actions and gestures.

Other than this parable in action that the exegetes have no doubts about, we have already recorded other parables of Jesus in action: sitting at table with sinners, the call of Levi the publican, the conversation with the Samaritan woman, the healing of the paralytic to show that Jesus could forgive sins, the bent over woman he healed on the Sabbath day.

I now invite you to reflect on the observation that Matthew makes about Jesus healing so many of the sick:

> That evening they brought to him many who were possessed with demons; and he cast out the spirits with a word and cured all who were sick. This was to fulfil what had been spoken through the prophet

Isaiah, 'He took our infirmities and bore our diseases' (8:16-17).

The significance of the miracles is not exhausted through physical healing: they are signs of *Jesus' tenderness and compassion*. We could say they are parables of his kindness.

Jesus himself (I am asking you to make this leap of faith) is a sign, a parable of God's tenderness for our lost, sick, weak and suffering humanity. We gradually come to contemplate Jesus as a parable of the Father's mercy: he did not limit himself to telling the parables of the merciful Father, but expresses the fact throughout his life, symbolises it, makes it real in a figurative way.

The Synoptics offer just a few points to support our claim, while John the Evangelist expresses it with absolute clarity:

> Philip said to him, 'LORD, show us the Father and we will be satisfied.' Jesus said to him, 'Have I been with you all this time, Phillip, and you still do not know me? Whoever has seen me has seen the Father. How can you say, "Show us the Father?" Do you not believe that I am in the Father and the Father is in me? The words that I say to you I do not speak on my own; but the Father who dwells in me does his works. Believe me that I am in the Father and the Father is in me; but if you do not, then believe me because of the works themselves' (14:8-11).

'I have been with you all this time' he wants to say: you have seen me act, speak, preach, heal and you should have understood that I am the sign, the presence of the Father's mercy, that I am the transparency of the Father! John goes further because he says *parable,* also *presence* and *transparency.*

Again, in the Fourth Gospel, towards the end of the Last Supper discourse, Jesus states:

> I have said these things to you in figures of speech. The hour is coming when I will no longer speak to you in figures but will tell you plainly of the Father. On that day you will ask in my name. I do not say to you that I will ask the Father on your behalf; for the Father himself loves you because you have loved me and have believed that I came from God. I came from the Father and have come into the world; again, I am leaving the world and am going to the Father (16:25-28).

The healing of the man born blind, the raising of Lazarus, the multiplication of the loaves, the conversation with the Samaritan woman, were all ways of saying: the Father loves you. I have come from the Father and am returning to the Father to bring you with me.

Jesus' entire life; his behaviour with the people, his way of loving can be described broadly as a parable of the Father. John the Evangelist himself invites us to make this leap of faith.

The parable of the pierced side

A question might arise here: in Jesus' life is there one action, one gesture presented as the high point of parable, where the mystery of the Father is revealed in a concise and eloquent way?

I argue that this high point in John's Gospel is *the pierced heart of Jesus*. We find ourselves before a very important passage, one John himself highlights for us:

> Since it was the day of Preparation, the Jews did not want the bodies left on the cross during the sabbath, especially because that sabbath was a day of great solemnity. So, they asked Pilate to have the legs of the crucified men broken and the bodies removed. Then the soldiers came and broke the legs of the first and of the other who had been crucified with him. But when they came to Jesus and saw that he was already dead, they did not break his legs. Instead, one of the soldiers pierced his side with a spear and at once blood and water came out. (*He who saw this has testified so that you also may believe. His testimony is true and he knows he tells the truth*). These things occurred so that the scripture might be fulfilled. 'None of his bones shall be broken.' And again, another passage of scripture says, 'They will look on the one whom they have pierced' (19:31-37).

It is clear that the Evangelist intended to focus meaning here. There are four points emphasising the importance of the fact that 'He who saw this has testified [1] so that you may also believe [2]}. His testimony is true [3] and he knows he tells the truth [4].' I find no other passage where John is quite saying: Attention! This is important, this is true, I am testifying to it. He very clearly wants to *focus the reader's attention on the sight of the pierced side.*

Then he notes: 'So that you may also may believe.' In truth, this subordinate clause is the purpose of the whole Fourth

Gospel: '... but these are written *so that you may come to believe*' (20:31). The entire Gospel can be read precisely by starting from the culminating sight that should open the eyes of faith to the contemplative gaze.

Seeing the piercing of the side, John grasps the heart of the gospel and can then put his book in order: it is a kind of key to reading the entire evangelical account.

I would like to point to some other elements that show the importance of this final scene.

In the prologue (1:14)

> And the Word became flesh and lived among us, and we have seen his glory, the glory as of a father's only son, *full of grace and truth.*
>
> *From his fullness we have all received, grace upon grace.* The law indeed was given through Moses, *grace and truth came through Jesus Christ.* No one has even seen God. It is God the only Son, who is close to the Father's heart, who has made him known (1:16-18).

So, Jesus reveals the Father.

If we were to ask John: 'When did you see his glory?' he would begin by answering: throughout his life somewhat, especially in the miracles, starting with Cana. But at Cana, even Jesus said his hour had not yet come. His hour is the hour of his passion and death, and it is at this point that the *prayer of glorification* is recorded:

> The hour has come for the Son of Man to be glorified. Very truly, I tell you, unless a grain of

wheat falls into the earth and dies, it remains just a single grain; but if it dies, it bears much fruit.

There is the glory, the moment of glorification:

'….. it is for this reason that I have come to this hour. Father, glorify your name.' Then a voice came from heaven, 'I have glorified it and I will glorify it again.' '….. Now is the judgement of this world; now the ruler of this world will be driven out. And I, when I am lifted up from the earth, will draw all people to myself.' He said this to indicate the kind of death he was to die (*12:23* and *27:31-33*).

John's statement in the prologue: 'we have seen his glory', is certainly true for the anticipation of glory, but especially true for the cross. The glory of the Father's only son, full of grace and truth, is what John contemplated when Jesus, 'having loved his own who were in the world, [he] loved them to the end' (Jn 13:1). These words, said at the washing of the feet, are symbolic of the supreme gesture of life given for all human beings.

It is also interesting to note that in John 19, speaking of the thrust of the spear and the blood and water shed, the Evangelist – who usually does not refer to passages from the Old Testament by contrast with Matthew, for example – quotes two passages from Scripture, with allusions to many others: 'None of his bones shall be broken' is a fusion of a verse from Psalm 34 with Isaiah 63, and alludes to a ritual prescription found in Exodus 12. 'They will look on the one they have pierced' is taken from Zechariah 12, where the prophet is speaking of a great restoration and support for the one who has been killed. So, it is a passage replete with mystery and symbols, and John has placed the high point of revelation and the passion within it. Seeing the blood and water flow from Jesus' heart, his gaze widens and he understand that he is the Paschal Lamb, the true Passover of the people, therefore the composite of all of Israel's worship and liturgy, brought to perfect fulfilment. He understands that Jesus is the righteous man who was persecuted, whom God supports, and who goes to his death for us all. Jesus, whom all people will look to, is the salvation of the world.

The blood and water, too, are clearly a parable, a puzzle, a symbol; a symbol of life and death in the first place: John contemplates the resurrection in death. Probably water and blood are the duality of *truth and grace* recalled in the prologue, and symbols of Messianic fullness: grace on grace, grace and truth, are messianic gifts in prophetic language. Blood is love poured out to the point of death, gracious love freely given. Water is the symbol of clear, luminous truth.

Water and blood are the graces God pours into human beings when he passes from death to life.

The piercing of the side reveals to us everything God is for humanity, the extent to which he loves us, and how human beings are filled with grace by this love, how in contemplation of the Christ we see the glory of the Father by becoming one with him.

It seems, then, that we can claim that the moment in which Jesus is most perfectly the parable of the Father, the expression of the mysterious, hidden love of God for sinful, suffering, solitary and condemned humanity, is when his heart is pierced by the spear. The Fathers of the Church, and the medieval mystics, cast their nets widely into this image because of its biblical roots. Pius XII's Encyclical *Haurietas*

Aquas marvellously developed the biblical sources of this contemplation of God's love that to a degree sums up our whole journey.

Looking at the world from the Cross

Let us finish with a brief practical reflection on the importance of looking at things from the heart of Christ on the cross. In this regard, I recall a very beautiful book by Sertillanges: *Ció che Gesù vedeva dall'alto della croce*. (What Jesus saw from up on the cross). What does it mean to look at things from up on the cross and, in particular, to interpret the situation of the Church on the 20th anniversary of Vatican Council II, while thinking of all its problems: post-conciliar problems, problems of the mission, the efforts the Church is making, the good or not so good?

It means two things especially:

1. *The first*: to view the world, history, our community, our personal pastoral problems, having understood something of the Father's *profound mercy*. It means to look at things, having understood the profound mercy of God for humanity. Then it means seeking to understand how all of history is only the history of God, who draws human beings to himself in the embrace of the cross, to unite them to the fullness of the Father. Everything flows from this, the open kerygma that is the strong proclamation of God's love flows from it, as does the hidden kerygma of the parables we have sought to understand the meaning of during these days. All the power of love until Christ's death, revealing the mystery of the Father's profound love, his profound mercy, flows from it. It means looking at things after having understood that the

serious mercy of God is the root of and key to human history, the Church's history, the history of our community's life.

2. *The second:* to view all human realities from the heart of Christ crucified, with the judgement that God's serious mercy makes of them. It means applying this especially to the situation of the post-conciliar Church (what has happened, whether we have gone forward or backward, who has understood it or who has understood it badly, or misunderstood it). It means not making a judgement only on doctrines or situations, but *to consider individuals in a loving way,* to consider the Church's journey in the light of God's mercy, including in the parables of judgement.

Only this kind of gaze can give the right tone to a judgement that, without descending into barren pessimism or superficial optimism, considers what the real journey of poor people is - and we all know it! It is a journey drawn step by step, irresistibly, mercifully, by the power of Christ's love flowing from the cross, a love that every human being can also, unfortunately and sadly, resist.

This is the gaze that constantly positions us correctly, that leads to the contemplation of history as Christ is contemplating it, making us a part of his judgement, a judgement not made once and for all, but which is the merciful action that continuously reminds humanity to accept his message.

We are called to be collaborators of this message, and must especially beg for the grace of a sublime understanding of Christ's cross.

PARABLES OF THE CALL

We will follow the same order as we have used for the other groups to meditate on the parables of the call: Which are they? What are they basically saying? What kind of people are they addressed to and what is in the heart of Jesus who is telling them? Finally, we will look at two applications stemming from them: mission and vocation ministry/activity.

Call and invitation

- What first comes to mind is the parable of the banquet, found in the double tradition of Matthew (22:1-13) and Luke. We will read it in Luke 14:15-24, because the whole chapter revolves around our theme:

> One of the dinner guests, on hearing this, said to him, 'Blessed is anyone who will eat bread in the kingdom of God!' Then Jesus said to him, 'Someone gave a great dinner and invited many. At the time for the dinner he sent his slave to say to those who had been invited, "Come, for everything is ready now." But they all alike began to make excuses. The first said to him, "I have bought a piece of land, and I must go out and see it; please accept my regrets." Another said, "I have bought five yoke of oxen, and I am going to try them out; please accept my regrets." Another said, "I have just been married and therefore cannot come." So, the slave returned

and reported this to the master. Then the owner of the house became angry and said to his slave, "Go out at once into the streets and lanes of the town and bring in the poor, the crippled, the blind and the lame." And the slave said, "Sir, what you ordered has been done, and there is still room." Then the master said to the slave, "Go out into the roads and lanes, and compel people to come in, so that my house may be filled. For I tell you, none of those who were invited will taste my dinner."'

The parable is so rich that many elements remind us of others. The rejection by some and acceptance by others reminds us, for example, of the different kinds of seed (eaten, smothered, matures, produces). The invitation extended to the poor, blind and lame, makes us think of going out to look for the lost. The final words, 'None of those who were invited will taste my dinner', remind us of the parables of judgement.

Nevertheless, it seems clear to me that the central theme is the invitation, the call, embarrassment at refusing the invitation, the miserly excuses justifying the refusal, the generosity of the one who continues to invite without tiring of it. Beside this fundamental parable of call, we can list others which, though not having the same structure, touch on the same issue:

- *Matthew 20:1-16*: engaging labourers for the vineyard at different hours. There is the owner who calls and then, in handing out wages, focuses more on his generosity than the work to be done. The emphasis here, then, is on the magnanimity of the owner and the graciousness of his call.

- *Matthew 21:28-32*: the tiny parable of the two sons (very little used because it is so dangerous!). One son says,

'I will go' and does not go; the other says 'I will not go' and does. They are different responses to their father's call. He offers an invitation, gives a command, makes a request. Who really listened to the call? The one who in fact went, not the one who said yes.

- *Luke 14:12-14*: this is a wisdom saying but needs to be cited because of its affinity with our theme:

> He said also to the one who had invited him, 'When you give a luncheon or a dinner, do not invite your friends or your brothers or your relatives or rich neighbours, in case they may invite you in return, and you would be repaid. But when you give a banquet, invite the poor, the crippled, the lame and the blind. And you will be blessed because they cannot repay you, for you will be repaid at the resurrection of the righteous.'

If we take the point of view of the one inviting and his generosity, we are within the framework of call, a freely offered call that expects no return payment. He awaits a response but gains nothing from it.

- *Matthew 13:44-46*: the parables of the hidden treasure and the pearl. The discovery of the treasure and the pearl is a unique, providential opportunity and carried with it responsibility for a call: What will I do now? How will I respond? Get on with it. Go and sell what you have!

- *Luke 14:28-33*: in this context I would add the building of the tower, and the war. Whoever wants to build a tower must first estimate the costs. Whoever wants to go to war is careful not to start out with too few men. What is this trying to say? Whoever wants to follow Jesus must renounce everything, must count the cost of such following. These are two small parables that point to the total decision needed to follow Jesus' invitation. This makes a parable of the historic invitation to the rich young man. The *rich young man* represents a typical scene of invitation with conditions for following Jesus: 'Go, sell what you own and give the money to the poor' (Mk 10:21). It is in strict parallel with the hidden treasure in the field, the precious pearl, the building of the tower, and the war. The call comes from a free heart and it involves the whole person. It demands we leave everything. This is why people instinctively defend themselves: I've taken a wife, bought fields, oxen ... Only the one who is poor in spirit willingly accepts: 'Blessed are the poor for theirs is the kingdom of heaven.'

- *Luke 10:29-37*: the parable of the Good Samaritan. At the beginning of our meditation, I said I did not know where to place it and, in fact, it is a separate story because of its magnificence. But in order to link it to others (not connections made *a priori* but an attempt to give some order to the many things Jesus said in many different circumstances), it seems to me that the encounter with the injured man is a call, an occasion of invitation. Do you want to be his neighbour? One says no, another likewise, and a third says yes. To be a neighbour means forgetting about the road you are on, leaving your journey, getting down, out, off to look after your brother or sister, and showing mercy. Although the words are different, as are also the circumstances of the call, call and the commandment of love are still there, nevertheless.

These are the parables of call: nine in all. Among other things, we have gone through almost all of Jesus' parables. Missing are a few that are difficult to classify; perhaps we could call them parables of prayer, the insistence on prayer. They are: *the importune friend* (Lk 11:5 ff.); *the unjust judge and the widow* (Lk 18:1-8), along with some comparisons: 'Is there anyone among you who, if your child asks for a fish, will give a snake .... Or if the child asks for an egg, will give a scorpion?' (Lk 11:9-13; Mt 7:7-11). These comparisons come close to the language of parable.

A further four parables do not fit into any classification and once again this shows how Jesus did not feel bound to any scheme and spoke in the language that to him seemed best suited to the real situation. Thus we have:

- The parable of the children in the market place singing and dancing, while others wilfully choose not to sing and dance (Mt 11:16-19; Lk 7:31-35).
- The return of the evil spirit in strength because he cannot return to the house unless the one stronger than him has been tied up (Mt 12:43-45; cf. *12:29-30*).
- The servant who returns home from work and has to prepare lunch for his master and serve him; similarly, those who do what they have to do must say at the end: 'We are worthless slaves' (Lk 17:7-10).
- The parable about first places at table. It could also be taken as a wisdom saying: 'When you are invited, go and sit down at the lowest place, so that when the host comes, he may say to you, 'Friend, move up higher" (Lk 14:7-10).

Characteristics of the invitation

What are the parables of the call saying? Beginning with the most important one, the banquet, I will list some characteristics that may help us to better appreciate Jesus' thinking.

1. *The kingdom of God is festive, precious, joyful*: it is similar to a banquet, a treasure, a wonderful pearl.

2. *Entrance to the banquet is not free; an invitation is needed*: a master calls, a king invites. Those invited are faced with a situation of responsibility and choice. The invitation is an act of grace, and the one inviting wants to spread his joy, manifest it, share it.

3. *The invitation is serious, and demanding.* There is strong emphasis on this. It is an invitation of love that involves life and seriously so. What is clear is the quality gap between the human and the divine. A human invitation can be accepted or rejected. There is no great harm done if refused; we are not existentially involved if it is accepted. Instead, God is so mysterious and wonderful that by inviting us he involves us, and it is an involvement, a commitment that changes our life, transfigures and reviews it.

4. *Whoever refuses the invitation is a fool and lacking in common sense.* Whoever does not go to the king's banquet puts forward pretexts because he knows he will offend the king, knows he has made a mistake and is not reasoning properly. He acts like a fool.

5. *Whoever refuses, legitimises his response.* Human beings tend to legitimise their rejection of God's Word, his call. Even when it is a case of simple calls expressing the kingdom in daily events, those who reject them always find excuses that seem to be good ones. People are ashamed to say: 'I said no to the Word of God.' They prefer to say that their 'no' is due to external situations: it is not the right moment; later, not

now, there's something urgent I have to do.... The parable here scrutinises the murky depths of the psyche that always rationalises what it is doing to show good reasons.

6. *The invitation is freely extended.* An invitation is needed because entry is not free in that sense, but nor is it reserved for an elite. It is addressed to the poor, the lame, everyone. We saw it in the search for the lost; here it is brought under the theme of invitation: all the unfortunate types are invited, the poor, and not only the gifted, wise, intelligent, noble. The parable starts with these because it has a human basis, then goes beyond this and reveals that the king, the master wants everyone, even the most wretched. So, there is no church of the elite but a church for everyone, without distinction and the invitation is made early, later and even at the final hour, at any hour. Generously. The wage the vineyard owner gives those who come in the final hour indicates that basically the work did not matter to the owner, but the fact that the individual responded and went away happy. As we were saying, the master's generosity, the lack of distributive justice always creates difficulties for us when we have to explain this parable.

7. *The invitation demands obedience and detachment.* The characteristic recalls the third point; a serious and demanding invitation. Here, however, it is deeper: it is not enough to say 'yes' in words. The son who said 'no', but still went, was obedient. Outside the language of parable are Jesus' words: 'It is not the one who says Lord, Lord, who will enter the kingdom of heaven, but the one who does the will of my Father' (Mt 7:21). The invitation demands a total response: whoever finds the treasure must sell everything he has, and

whoever finds the pearl sells everything in order to buy it. It demands seriousness because we cannot build a house without being serious about it; one cannot go to war without careful preparation. Responding to the invitation brings consequences that bite into life.

8. *The invitation is near you, unexpected, just around the corner.* The Samaritan was not waiting to discover the invitation. At a certain moment the call intervenes: Do you want to be a neighbour? Do you want to love your neighbour? Then you must do such and such, otherwise you don't love your neighbour. It is not just a generic invitation to faith: clearly there is this too, but it is specified in all the situations of serious responsibility presented to us by life and that are opportunities, but also possibilities for failure.

Kingdom business

What kind of people does the narrator of these parables have before him?

1. *People who know what business is all about is,* recognise good opportunities in life. However, they believe that 'business' is all about daily matters: money, houses, consumer goods, things of current concern. So, they think that kingdom business is not so important. These are people who need a good shake up, who have to understand: pay attention, because you will lose out on the real deal due to your business concerns; you will miss out on the fundamental chance of your lifetime, the unique and unrepeatable opportunity for human fullness, and your salvation. It is an audience that needs to be involved in the discourse that belongs to parable:

these people who refused the invitation to the king's banquet are rude and have made a mistake! And you?

They could easily have gone to see their oxen a day later; without putting off their purchase altogether. They could have just postponed it for such an important and kindly offered invitation. And you?

2. *People who think the Christian vocation is just one among many*, similar to all the others. Vocation is not 'the thing' for them, not 'the business' that does not suffer or admit confusion with any other. Hence, the need to insist on the serious nature of its demands: faith involves our whole life, all of our being, the whole person. 'Love the Lord with all your heart, and with all your soul, and with all your mind and all your strength' (Mk 12:30).

The kingdom involves the whole person, and based on this fundamental insight, other things can find their place. It is not enough to have just a little bit of religion, mass on Sundays, a little bit of human honesty, a little bit of prayer, amusement, all measured out.

We can appreciate, then, how relevant the public listening to the parables of the call is, and how we find this public so much within us! We are the beneficiaries of these parables, we must feel ourselves involved because it is so easy for so many things in our life, our day, not to be in accord with the serious nature of Jesus' demands.

'Lord, grant that we may understand that here and now we are the ones to whom these parables are addressed and that the theme of the call is above all for us. Lord, you who call us, grant that we may grasp the seriousness, uniqueness the exigency, the categorical and total nature of our baptismal call. And may we realise that our vocational call then makes our baptismal call explicit in the Church in an historical, personal and ministerial way.'

Invitation to the wedding

What does Jesus have in his heart as he tells the parables of the call? It seems to me that we can read three convictions especially in his heart:

1. *The person speaking thus is convinced that preaching the gospel is a most valuable opportunity for the human being,* one not comparable with any other. Jesus is convinced that the gospel means assent to the gospel, faith, justice, holiness. It is an offer to human freedom not to be lost at any cost, because it is our true good.

2. *The person speaking thus has a great sense of the completeness that God is for the human being,* and so, one cannot say no to God who calls. Jesus knows that the God of love is the one who completes and realises the human being. God is our fullness.

3. There is another truth which it seems to me must be read in Jesus' heart, even if it is not said quite so directly in the parables, because they speak especially of the Father.

The person telling these parables has the divine and messianic authority to say: 'Follow me!' and to establish the conditions: whoever follows me and does not renounce their own life cannot be my disciple. In the context of the entire gospel it is clear that here Jesus is the Messiah, Son of Man, and Son of God, the Lord of human history, the one who can call people in human history. For us there is something more. The parables present the theme of the banquet, but also the wedding banquet. So, we need to say that, in the New Testament context, not only can and does the Lord call in history – he has called and continues to call me, but it is the bridegroom who is inviting me to the wedding, inviting me into intimacy; 'Listen! I am standing at the door, knocking …. I will come in to you and eat with you and you with me' (Rev 3:20).

'Lord, grant that I may read you this way in my life and understand the chance, the impressive and providential opportunity that the call, my vocation, is for my life. It is where your historic, unrepeatable and powerful appeal to me is expressed in the context of the Church and its possibility of calling people.'

Mission and vocation work and ministry

We can draw two consequences from the meditation:

1. The first concerns the *missionary nature of the Church and of individuals in the Church.* Where does the missionary impetus that characterises the Church and is an essential part of it, come from?

a) In individuals, it comes first of all from the sense of the precious nature of the *'bonum fidei'*, the good of the Faith, from the certainty that the Faith is worth more than everything else. The Faith is the supreme good for me and for others because it is the foundation and root of complete, total salvation for the human being. The missionary impulse comes from our depth of faith, liveliness of faith, from the joy, effort of faith and from suffering for the Faith. It is proclamation of the Faith.

b) Secondly, considering faith in itself, not individual faith, we can say that the missionary impulse comes from the fact that since faith is a 'good', of its nature it asks to be spread, especially faith lived out in charity, love. If the Church is love and the love that comes of faith, this love can only but be spread, can only but communicate itself: it is the intrinsic communicability of faith as a good that becomes the desire in people to communicate it if they live by faith as individuals. This is why the Church as a community of faith is missionary, an open and expansive place. A Christian community cannot content itself with saying: we have been given the gift of faith. Praise the Lord! If it is a true Christian community, it must experience the need to spread faith everywhere, in everything.

Already before Vatican II, Pius XI, in his Encyclical on the missions, wrote: 'As a matter of fact, this type of charity surpasses all other kinds of good works inspired by love just as the mind surpasses the body, heaven surpasses earth, eternity surpasses time. Every one that acts thus, inspired by love and according to the full measure of his ability, demonstrates that he esteems the gift of faith in the manner that one should esteem it.' Propagating the Faith is the first duty of Christianity, it is the greatest charity; all the other works of charity are tied to and subordinate to this highest work. The deeper our faith, then, the more it is rooted in us and expressed in love, the more we are missionaries. Depth of faith does not necessarily mean to say a peaceful faith or one that poses no problems; rather does it mean struggling for faith, love for faith, darkness of faith, the desert of faith, a desert where the human being feels even more that faith is their salvation, fullness, the totality of self, and where the individual feels unable to define themselves without it.

2. *The second consequence concerns vocation work, ministry.* Where does the vocational impetus come from? It comes, as does faith, from the deep, personal and community awareness that vocation is of enormous worth, that it is the supreme good in which the gift of faith is realised for the individual. It is realised for me and for others.

The vocational impetus, then, has nothing to do with the notion of human propaganda, the sense of ambition to increase the number of members of our congregation, or the desire not to die alone but to see the faces of new brothers or sisters in religion. What counts is my vocation, the place where I have found the fullness of the cross and life, which is why I want it to count for others. Vocation will then be proposed as the highest good seen in the light of God, not as an urge, a trap (come and see how good you will find it, there are lots of things you'll like …).

Perhaps we can respond to the question so often asked today: why are there so few vocations? Evidently because some have taken a wife, bought a field, have to go and see their oxen: excuses, then, justification, refusal on the part of those who have received the call. And then, perhaps, because the call is weak. Both these are part of it. It is not enough to say that young people are not very generous. We need to add that perhaps our religious or priestly life is not lived joyfully, enthusiastically, with the fullness of love for the cross, with complete dedication, shining example, the strength and force of unity and love, with the perception that we really become holy in the community.

Let us reflect seriously on this and ask the Lord to translate the parable of the call for us, for me. We should not be afraid to ask ourselves: why is my calling of others so weak? I do my duty well, I try to serve generously, yet I feel ill at ease having to call others. Why? If we put all our good will into clarifying these motives for ourselves, the Lord will give us the gift of new light for ourselves and others.

PARABLE, EUCHARIST, LIFE IN THE SPIRIT

'Lord, grant that
we may gain some fruits from your Word.
May your Word
also enlighten
our understanding of life in the Church
and our life in the Church.'

At the conclusion of our work over these days, I would like to offer a meditation that could be given the title: Parable, Eucharist, Life in the Spirit. Naturally, it is not possible to deal extensively with such a huge topic. I will restrict myself to pointing out some relationships, some of the connections between these things that can be considered from a unified perspective, beginning with the parables and *with parable as such*. I refer to a passage from Mark where Jesus is scolding the disciples who have not understood the parable of the seed, saying: 'Do you not understand *this parable? Then how will you understand all parables?*' (Mk 4:13).

By turning these words of Jesus around, we could say that whoever understands this parable understands all the parables, because they are threaded together like the pearls of a necklace. By seeking to penetrate ever more into the linguistic and historical dynamic of the language of parable, parable in action, we arrive at the shores of symbolic language and symbolic actions that become sacraments. The sacraments are symbolic and efficacious gestures, signs.

We have contemplated Jesus who sheds blood and water from on the cross, to indicate death and resurrection, the fullness of life and love, the richness of grace which is the Church, the sacraments. Blood and water are the sublime, living parable of God's love for human beings. It is the contemplation of Easter, the centre, the central point of reference for all Christian experience.

Now, we could ask ourselves how to make Easter present, how to act in a way that it is not only contemplation of the gospel text, of what happened in the past and still has value for the present, but so that the pierced heart of Christ can enter our daily existence, *here and now*. Jesus provides the answer and it is recorded by St Paul: 'For as often as you eat this bread and drink the cup, you proclaim the Lord's death until he comes' (1 Cor 11:26); proclaim Easter, proclaim it. The Eucharist is the kerygma in action, a living presence at the heart of the Church, at the heart of Christian life, and the sublime parable of God's love for humankind that is Christ crucified while shedding blood and water from his pierced side.

Parable and Eucharist

In what way is the Eucharist related to parable and parable in action? What did Christ want to say in real terms? What does it mean for Christian life, our daily life, especially for a Church about to celebrate a Eucharistic Congress?

1. *First of all, the Eucharist is an action.* Jesus' command, recorded in the First Letter to the Corinthians, is 'Do it', not

'Say it'. We often speak of the Eucharist almost as if it were a *thing* and not an *action*. It is rightly said that the Eucharist is a person: in the Eucharist Jesus is present in his body, blood, soul and divinity under the species of bread and wine. However, it is made present in an *historical action* of the Church. It is not simply an epiclesis: putting the bread and wine on the altar and saying: 'Come Lord' and the Lord comes. We are re-doing the supper, repeating the words of Jesus, making gestures, movements, preparing to eat the body of Jesus and drinking his blood. All this together is the Eucharist. It is a true historical deed with its times and gestures.

From here, we can better grasp the analogy between the Eucharistic celebration and the power and value of parable in action. The parable in action is an historical action with higher meaning: Jesus curses the barren fig tree, the fig tree withers, and this is a sign of God's judgement. The Eucharist celebrated is an historical action of the Church: its coming together, sitting down at the table, saying Jesus' words, breaking bread do not only signify but they *make happen* the greatest event in history, Easter – cross, death, resurrection. Hence, the Church carries out the signs, gestures, actions in which Jesus signified his death out of love, and by doing so, makes it present.

The Eucharist is to be understood through these relationships, these actions, parallels: the action of the Church which repeats Jesus' supper, the supper that anticipated the cross. It is the action of the Church that proclaims the cross and its meaning. Our catechesis should always range between Eucharist as celebration (gestures, prayers, words, movements), Jesus' supper (with its gestures, words, prayers), and the cross as the supreme moment of Jesus' gift to us, already present in the supper under the symbol of bread and wine offered to the disciples as his body and blood. The bread and wine offered, signify a higher reality, signify the body and blood given by Jesus on the cross to show the world the infinite love of the Father. The Eucharist is certainly a mystery that is lost in the infinity of God, but when we move through it lovingly – meditating on the supper or contemplating the cross, or celebrating it – we experience and live out the fundamental moment of history and are involved in it.

2. *The involvement recalls another characteristic of the parables.* The parable, we have said, is not neutral, and draws the listener in. Equally, the Eucharist celebrated by the Church in the memory and repetition of the supper that signifies the gift of the cross, involves whoever takes part in it. It calls on us not only to receive the body and blood of Christ, but to also do what Jesus did. Effectively it calls on us to give our body and blood for our brothers and sisters, 'Do this in memory of me' as a celebratory memorial; 'Do this' in life. In fact, the real fruit of the Eucharist is charity, the perfection of the gift of life. The Eucharist, besides effectively making Jesus present to adore, puts the energy of love in the heart of the person participating in it. One could also say: the real fruit of the Eucharist is the Holy Spirit inasmuch as he is the uniting power of the community's love, the uniting and expansive power of love, love radiating outwards.

While we welcome the Holy Spirit in Confirmation as the power of witness, complementing our baptismal consecration, in the Eucharist we welcome the gift of the Holy Spirit as the fire of charity. And because charity is God's very essence, the definition of God, the most sublime reality that exists, the highest perfection of our humanity, the Eucharist is the most sublime sacrament, the culmination of Christian life and – as Vatican II says – the high point of evangelisation. It is so because it proclaims the perfect love of God for humankind in the love of Christ who gives himself on the cross and through the real presence of the person of Jesus it efficaciously brings about the transformation of the assembly into a community of charity and love.

The Eucharist is the proclamation of the kerygma in its highest expressive form, proclaiming the fact of the kerygma and its efficacy, bringing us human beings together to be unity in love.

Significance of the Eucharistic Congress

A Eucharistic Congress should proclaim the Eucharist in its glory as an effective sign of the world renewed. A Eucharistic Congress should show that from the primacy of charity, from the Eucharistic gift of the spirit of love, come all the other expressions of Christian life: the sacraments, the commandments, institutions, all the social, charitable, ministerial nature of the community. In 1983 when we celebrated the National Eucharistic Congress in Milan, it was proposed that we focus on 'the centre' because, in fact, it is difficult to think of two themes. By saying, 'Eucharist *and* family', for example, we risk either speaking about marriage with all the problems it presents (understanding between spouses, education of children, etc.) or speaking about the Eucharist as adoration.

A Eucharistic Congress, by definition, focuses on *the Eucharist*. Naturally one can consider a second element, a second theme. But all the effort should go into explaining that from the centrality of the Eucharist flows the given aspect of Christian life. This requires lengthy preparation, reflection and prolonged contemplation.

In our case, it is about showing in particular that the power of the sap of Eucharistic love flourishes in the context of the couple and the family. There is no lack of indications in the New Testament. I am thinking of the never sufficiently explored text in Ephesians 5 which speaks of Jesus and the Church. St Paul says: 'Husbands, love your wives, just as Christ loved the Church and gave himself up for her' (Eph 5:25). 'Gave' ('*parédoke*') is the typical verb in his passion and death, hence it recalls the whole mystery of the passion as the Father's love, the Son's love, despite human beings putting Jesus to death, and it highlights Jesus' love for humanity. It is an important point of departure for understanding the relationship between Easter, the gift of Christ to the Church, and matrimony as a parable of Christ's love for the Church, as an efficacious, historical concrete sign of the fundamental reality that is Christ's love for the Church expressed in all its power in the Eucharist.

A problem arises here, naturally. This visual scene of marriage, the family, is very beautiful, but the reality is so different! Married life is full of difficulties, dark moments, struggles (finances, etc). If marriage is a sign of the love Christ has for his Church, why, in practice, does it not succeed in being experienced that way? Have we made a mistake? Do we need to have less sublime ideals, or need to be content with aiming at just a minimum of conditions for its dignity? If ideals are too high, they do not function, e.g. when the husband is a drunkard or the wife is tired or the children are sick! And that is without naming poverty, lack of employment, and so many other things that give rise to misunderstanding in the family.

It is necessary to reflect on these questions in the week dedicated to 'Eucharist and the family', otherwise these two things will always be a bit disconnected even at the level of awareness. On the one hand, the highest Eucharistic ideal, which only some couples achieve (if they do!), is encouraged by privileged conditions – culture, education, tradition – and on the other hand, by going forward with rather difficult criteria.

'Lord,' we should ask, 'how does this come about? Have we perhaps exaggerated in building up these images, or do we have too little faith, not believing in the power of the Gospel that can transform human life? Or have we unwittingly transferred our western traditions into the ideal picture of family and spousal life and said what the Scriptures do not say?'

I add here a reflection that is also valid for other problems of Christian life. Often, we paint a certain ideal picture of Christian life and then when we see the reality with all its difficult situations, we get confused and depressed. It seems to me that we need to grasp, in truth and fidelity, therefore in humble attention to the Word, the teaching of the gospel. We also need to understand what the merciful economy of salvation is as it patiently draws the poverty and fragility of the human experience toward the perfection of the sublime model. It is a mistake to have a static notion (here is the model, here is the practice), while it is correct to think that there is some focus drawing things to itself, a reality on the move that must be at the heart of this model to be itself, realising nevertheless that divine mercy draws things to itself gradually.

In other words, it is the relationship between the *open and hidden kerygma,* or parable, that we have so often called on over these days: they are both there but one does not destroy the other. The *hidden* kerygma, the parable, starts out from the open kerygma, but it presumes it is offered by a God who knows the human creature and makes his proposal mercifully, teaching gradual and patient ways for this creature to come to some fulfilment in history. If we were able to reflect more on these truths, we would gain greater peace with ourselves, with things and situations. Sometimes, we are caught in a dichotomy: the ideal 'could be' but it needs to be adapted; in the end, we are not content, and swing this way and that, without having grasped the link of attraction that joins the heart of Christ on the cross to all the rest of poor humanity, ourselves included. It is an unceasing, gradual attraction that we are called to encourage and accompany by defending the people from the backsliding ever at work through Satan's wiles and the dead-weight of worldliness.

Parable and life in the Spirit

The nexus between parable and life in the Spirit seems rather evident from what we have attempted to say about the Eucharistic mystery – St Paul speaks about life in the Spirit in the Letter to the Romans, Chapter 8:

> For the law of the Spirit of life in Christ Jesus has set you free from the law of sin and death ... but you are not in the flesh, you are in the Spirit, since the Spirit of God dwells in you... If you live according to the flesh you will die; but if by the Spirit you put to death the deeds of the body, you will live. For all

who are led by the Spirit of God are children of God ... You have received a spirit of adoption. When we cry, 'Abba! Father!' it is that very Spirit bearing witness that we are children of God.

Life according to the Spirit is the Christian life, insofar as it is enlivened, moved, attracted by the Spirit and insofar, therefore, as it is a life of love, joy, faith, hope, a life of the beatitudes, life of the Son of God, of sonship, trust, calling on God as Father with love, even in life's painful circumstances. Life according to the Spirit is life that identifies with Christ's tastes and choices through spiritual discernment. It comes from baptism and finds the climax of its strength in the Eucharist, its ongoing food. It finds its daily light and strength in reading and meditating on the Word.

We can ask ourselves: How does this life according to the Spirit become a living parable for the world? How is it a parable in action for the world?

We find the answer in some biblical texts, two of which are found in Matthew's Gospel:

> 'You are the salt of the earth; but if salt has lost its taste, how can saltiness be restored? It is no longer good for anything but is thrown out and tramped underfoot' (5:13).

We are warned, in language akin to parable, that as Christians sanctified by Baptism, nurtured by the Eucharist and moved by the Spirit, we are either salt for the world or we are nothing, worse than nothing.

Again:

> 'You are the light of the world. A city built on a hill cannot be hid. No one after lighting a lamp puts it under the bushel basket, but on the lampstand, and it gives light to all in the house. In the same way, let your light shine before others, so that they may see your good works and give glory to your Father in heaven' (5:14-16).

Here, the significance of life in the Spirit as a living parable is clear: it is light and, as such, must lead others, including non-believers, to glorify God by good works.

So life in the Spirit itself has an apostolic, missionary significance specified and explored in John's Gospel, where Jesus speaks of mutual love among the disciples – as the badge of their discipleship – and of unity among his own, as a sign by which the world will know that the Father has sent him. In this sense, the spiritual life of the Christian is a sign and stimulus for God's glory, a sign of the divine unity, divine love.

We come back to contemplation of Jesus' life as a parable of God's tenderness, and this is then entrusted to Christian life in the Spirit which is light, salt, an invitation to glorify, a city on the mountaintop that is a sign of discipleship in Christ and Christ's messianic mission in the world.

'Until all of us come to the unity of faith'

I would like to conclude with a practical reflection applicable to the life of individual Christians but especially applicable to community witness.

Personal Christian testimony is clearly most important: it is enough to think of the lasting efficacy of the lives of the saints.

Nevertheless, Jesus speaks of the testimony of the Church as Church, of his disciples loving one another, living in unity. A question arises spontaneously, parallel to the one we asked about marriage: how can we testify to unity, charity, if we are so divided? Sometimes this division saddens us to the point of being inwardly torn, and rightly so.

1. There is no greater scandal than division among Christians, among the baptised. This is why ecumenical yearning is part of the parabolic tension of life according to the Spirit. It is just as true that unity among Christians is the fundamental point, and that humanity called to baptism has partly failed Jesus' precept.

We could say that we Catholics are united, and that we are the true Church. However, there are baptised people (therefore people who are part of Christ and possibly even sharing in the Eucharist) who are divided, and this casts a shadow over history. Thus, it is right and proper to be very concerned, seriously and intelligently so, about ecumenism, especially in countries where division is more sensational. We need to adore, humble ourselves, pray, sigh, ask as Jesus did in the Garden of Gethsemane. He probably had something of this experience there, thinking of his disciples who were about to be scattered.

Unity concerns us as baptised Christians. Naturally, we should not undervalue the fact that as long as we are Catholics we have strong motivation for unity: only when there is a break from the Catholic Church is there division that is scandalous.

2. But we need to consider unity among ourselves, within our communities. It can be helpful to read some passages from the Letter to the Ephesians, Chapter 4, because it is good to encourage one another and also good to *encourage one another intelligently*. If we do not do so intelligently, we can fall into defeatism or cause ruptures: 'There is no unity', 'there is no community', 'nothing happens here', 'unity will never come about', 'it would be better to go home' .... These kinds of appeal to unity, community, charity show we have already lost confidence. Probably these poor results from a good start can be attributed to the fact that the notion has not been properly thought through, theologically and psychologically. The idea of unity taken globally is applied, that is, to situations that are but one aspect, one instance of Christian unity.

It is a recurring problem in the life of the Church, more so when often the unity invoked is a way of lamenting that things are not going the way we want, or because there is no unity *with me*. We should not marvel that even the most beautiful concepts, like unity, are badly employed or wasted. I recall, in this regard, some community meetings in the tumultuous 1970s, when it seemed necessary to renew everything, and ended up inevitably in useless anguish of conscience: no one here likes one another, everyone speaks badly of the others, there is no Christian charity, etc. Crying out about the lack of charity demonstrates that one does not have the true spirit of charity because one ends up acting toward the community in a disrespectful and offensive way. Words are not enough, deeds are needed; and deeds are not enough; the intelligence of faith is needed.

This is why I would like to turn to some beautiful pages in the Letter to the Ephesians: 'I therefore, the prisoner in the Lord, beg you to lead a life worthy of the calling to which you have been called, with all humility and gentleness, with patience, bearing with one another in love.'

Here, we already see which sentiments the appeal to unity is made of: St Paul does not begin by warning that they need to be united, but first of all encourages them in humility, gentleness, patience, understanding, bearing with one another. 'Making every effort to maintain the unity of the Spirit in the bond of peace.' *'Making every effort'* emphasises that it is not easy. The Greek text says *'spoudàzon'*, acting diligently: it is not a condition already achieved but one to be worked at and constantly retried. And after mentioning unity of the Spirit in the bond of peace, the Apostle describes what he means by unity:

> One body and one Spirit, just as you were called to the one hope of your calling, one Lord, one faith, one baptism, one God and Father of all, who is above all and through all and in all (4:1-6).

It is a threefold list, made up of three members each, nine elements that are the pillars of unity: 'One body [the one body of Christ], one Spirit, one hope, one Lord, one faith, one baptism.' At this point the panorama alters: 'One God and Father of all, who is above all and through all and in all.' Here unity broadens into a complex unity and becomes the unity that God works in the variety of people, gestures, situations.

First, God, being one, is above all, acts through all and is in all. The unity of the community is given by one God and by the one Spirit at work in everyone: as long as there is baptism, true faith, Eucharist, there is unity. Because, as I was saying, to lack unity is to fall away from the Catholic Faith, and so long as there is the Catholic Faith there is substantial unity, and it is a miracle of God that it exists. If we wish to build greater unity, we must start from what exists already and recognise that what is there is already an infinite gift of God.

Having begun to broaden unity in the direction of multiplicity, Paul then moves on to the variety of gifts, and this is the point he wanted to arrive at because the problem emerges from different gifts, charisms, ministries that do not manage to be in agreement:

> But each of us was given a grace according to the measure of Christ's gift. Therefore, it is said, 'When he ascended on high he made captivity itself a captive; he gave gifts to his people.' (When it says, 'He ascended,' what does it mean but that he had also descended into the lower parts of the earth? He who descended is one who ascended far above all the heavens so that he might fill all things) (vv. 7-10).

It seems that Paul is digressing: he wanted to speak of charisms, gifts, and all of a sudden he is speaking about Jesus who ascended and had previously descended! Perhaps, his heart burning with love for Jesus, the apostle begins speaking of the kerygma again without realising it. However, he probably intends to establish what he is about to say concerning unity in the primordial unity of Christ who, like God, descended into the depths to rise and bring all to unity.

> The gifts he gave were that some would be apostles, some evangelists, some pastors and teachers, to equip the saints for the work of ministry, for

building up the body of Christ, *until all of us come to the unity of faith and of the knowledge of the Son of God*, to maturity, to the measure of the full stature of Christ (vv. 11-13).

Paul's words astonish us, because it seems that unity has not yet come. Sometimes, some of our disappointments regarding unity come from the fact that we confuse final unity with the unity on the journey, along the way, that everyone is working at so everyone can come 'to the unity of faith and knowledge of the Son of God, to maturity, to the measure of the full stature of Christ.' This full maturity of Christ is not yet here; this body is immature, presents some childish signs, some tensions, difficulties, some squabbles. *This is how it is.* What is important is that it is on the way to full unity. From this perspective, the important thing is not to have perfect and total unity, but to make the constant effort to journey toward the full unity of the body of Christ that is the kingdom of God, is Christ at the moment he will present the kingdom to the Father. 'We must no longer be children, tossed to and fro and blown about by every wind of doctrine' (v. 14).

Sometimes, the 'false wind of doctrine' is a false idea of unity, for which, like children, we cling to an ideal which is not then matched by reality, and at that point we no longer know where best to start out from. '.... Tossed to and fro ... by people's trickery, by their craftiness, in deceitful scheming.' There is also trickery and craftiness in certain appeals to unity. 'But speaking the truth in love, we must grow up in every way into him who is the head, into Christ' (vv. 14-15).

In conclusion, it seems to me that St Paul is speaking of a threefold unity:

A. *There is the underlying unity* (one faith, one baptism, one God, one Lord) which is the indubitable, firm, total point of departure. If this comes into question, the Church is divided, there is heresy or apostasy.

B. *There is final unity:* 'until all of us come to the unity of the faith and of the knowledge of the Son of God, to maturity, to the measure of the full stature of Christ,' which is the perfect unity and harmony of the kingdom, the peace of the kingdom, the body of Christ come to maturity through the maturity of faith of people who have been purified by the trials of life and have learned to live in charity, peace, love, and thus live on for all eternity.

C. Between basic unity and final unity (needed as reference and model) *there is unity of action,* the commitment to constantly bringing the multiplicity of charisms, that comes from this very unity, back to growth toward perfect unity, hence to greater agreement, understanding, coordination including outward coordination, knowing, however, that we will never quite get there.

I recall the rather sceptical but very true comment of Cardinal Ballestrero's on the final day of the Loreto Church Congress: 'Let us remind ourselves that there will never be perfect reconciliation on this earth!' Here we are constantly on the way, constantly re-attempting reconciliation, in a state of ongoing forgiveness because we are in a state of ongoing deficiency and want.

How, then, can we be light and salt? Our responsibility is certainly a serious one, but I believe that those to whom God gives the light of faith, and not only a sociological outlook on the Church, can understand that there is a powerful basic unity, a marvellous final unity that people are working towards seriously, courageously to overcome things, forgive one another, understand one another, work together. There is a Church on the move to higher things, a Church carefully, keenly, courageously on the way to perfect communion of hearts. To say that we will change when everyone in the Church loves one another is an excuse, and is equivalent to saying, 'Lord, accept my regrets, I have to go and see the field I have bought, my oxen ...'

Unity along the way, if experienced intensely, is a sign that fulfils underlying and final unity, but if our steps are weak, if the journey onward is taken in simple resignation, then it becomes a countersign, and whoever sees it has the right to say that not only do these people not love one another, but they make no effort to do so!

'Lord, grant us the grace of being a sign of this charity and living this way among ourselves first of all, as we have done over the days. May this unity show itself in our lives through prayer, adoration, and contemplation of you.'

In a few days in Nairobi, crowds of people will be on their knees before *a piece of bread*. These people will come from many regions, nations, cultures, and will remain in humble and adoring silence before the Eucharist. What is urging these people if it is not the miracle, the power of Christian unity? It is a formidable power of unity not created by custom, culture or tradition, but by the power of faith – the basic unity that fixes its gaze on the final goal of unity and becomes, for those with eyes and ears, a sign capable of moving hearts.

>
> 'Lord,
> as we adore you together,
> may we serve you together.
> Grant that we may be able to be
> a sign of your unity,

testimony to fraternal charity, forgiveness, understanding and love for all humankind.'

CARLO MARIA MARTINI Foundation

The Carlo Maria Martini Foundation came into existence through the initiative of the Italian Province of the Jesuits and with the involvement of the Archdiocese of Milan.

It aims at remembering Cardinal Carlo Maria Martini by promoting knowledge and study of his life and works and keeping alive the spirit that animated his commitment, encouraging experience and knowledge of the Word of God in the context of our contemporary culture.

With this in mind, the Foundation's role is spelt out in a number of specific actions:

- Bringing the Cardinal's works, writings and addresses together in an archive and promoting their study as well as encouraging and authorising their publication.
- Supporting and nurturing ecumenical and inter-religious dialogue, with civil society and non-believers as well, working closely together to understand the indissoluble connection between faith, justice and culture.
- Fostering the study of Scripture involving other disciplines, including spirituality and social sciences.
- Contributing to pastoral and formative projects valuing Ignatian pedagogy and addressed especially to the young.
- Supporting study of the meaning and extended practice of the Spiritual Exercises.

Those who wish to can contribute to the collection of materials (written, audio, video) on Cardinal Martini by indicating initiatives regarding him by writing to
segretaria@fondazionecarlomariamartini.it

To subscribe to the newsletter (in Italian) and support the Foundation's activities: www.fondazionecarlomariamartini.it

BIBLICAL MEDITATIONS

A selection of sermons, retreats and meditation texts drawn from the vast work of Cardinal Martini. There is a roundup of biblical personalities from Old and New Testaments, explanations, some chosen topics to accompany reflections on the human being in search of God. The inestimable legacy of a man of prayer and contemporary spirituality.

1. **The Accounts of the Passion.** Meditations
2. **Paul.** In the midst of his ministry
3. **Our Father.** Do not heap up empty phrases
4. **The Apostles.** Men of peace and reconciliation
5. **Abraham.** Our father in faith
6. **Jesus.** Why he spoke in parables?
7. **Elijah.** The living God
8. **Stephen.** Servant and witness
9. **Peter.** Confessions
10. **Jacob.** A man's dream
11. **Jeremiah.** A prophetic voice in the city
12. **Israel.** A people on the move
13. **Samuel.** Religious and civil prophet
14. **Timothy.** Timothy's way

www.ingramcontent.com/pod-product-compliance
Lightning Source LLC
Chambersburg PA
CBHW030635150426
42811CB00077B/2113/J